DSM-III
TRAINING GUIDE
FOR DIAGNOSIS OF
CHILDHOOD DISORDERS

DSM-III
TRAINING GUIDE
FOR DIAGNOSIS OF
CHILDHOOD DISORDERS

By

Judith L. Rapoport, M.D.

and

Deborah R. Ismond, M.A.

Brunner/Mazel, *Publishers* • **New York**

Library of Congress Cataloging in Publication Data

Rapoport, Judith L., 1933–
    DSM-III training guide for diagnosis of childhood
disorders.

    Includes bibliographical references and index.
    1. Child psychopathology—Diagnosis. 2. Child
psychopathology—Classification. 3. Diagnostic and
statistical manual of mental disorders. 3rd ed.
I. Ismond, Deborah R., 1955-   . II. Title.
III. Title: D.S.M.-III training guide for child
psychiatry. IV. Title: DSM-3 training guide for child
psychiatry. [DNLM: 1. Mental disorders—In infancy
and childhood. 2. Mental disorders—Diagnosis. 3. Child
psychiatry—Nomenclature. WS 350 R219d]
RJ503.5.R36 1983   618.92'89075   83-18945
ISBN 0-87630-351-3

SECOND PRINTING

Copyright © 1984 by Judith L. Rapoport and Deborah R. Ismond

Published by
BRUNNER/MAZEL, INC.
19 Union Square
New York, New York 10003

MANUFACTURED IN THE UNITED STATES OF AMERICA

Contents

Introduction

The study of any type of phenomena requires a system for grouping and labeling events. In the mental health field, DSM-III is such a formulation. It intends to categorize descriptively clinical information, whether introspective, biological or social. Medical science has successfully employed a similar approach, and we hope that psychiatry will be equally rewarded in its endeavor to identify causes, predict outcomes, and establish effective treatments.

Opponents of this descriptive categorization argue that the diagnostic process may lead to erroneous conclusions about underlying biological or psychological handicaps. There is apprehension that the stigma of a psychiatric label leads to a self-fulfilling prophecy; such concern is expressed with particular vehemence when children are concerned. Evidence does exist indicating that a child's potential and ability are influenced by expectations and attitudes. However, the designation of a diagnostic term does not parallel the use of labels by the public to identify the deviant. A psychiatric explanation may, in some instances, ease social expectations and foster patience and encouragement in place of punishment and derision.

The diagnostic categories delineated in DSM-III attempt to systematically and comprehensively describe psychopathology as it is encountered in clinical practice. For the most part, it has successfully avoided making assumptions about underlying etiology and has focused on description of behavior.

Diagnosis serves several purposes as outlined clearly by Spitzer and Cantwell (1980). It first addresses the question, "Is there a disorder present and, if so, does it fit a known syndrome?" In addition to classification issues, diagnosis is important for identifying the influences on and possible causes of the disorder in terms of family conflict, biological endowment, and social roots. A complete case formulation also addresses the forces promoting normal development. A thorough evaluation is the key to answering diagnostic questions and to planning successful treatment.

This handbook offers further clarification and definition of the terms and concepts included in the DSM-III criteria for disorders pertaining specifically to children and adolescents. Although DSM-III devotes a section to psychopathology arising during these early years, other psychiatric disorders, such as anxiety, obsessive compulsive disorder, depression, and schizophrenia, also occur in childhood. The diagnostic criteria for these are largely the same for children and adults, but particular issues emerge when making differential diagnoses of these disorders in children.

It is our hope that use of this guide will help to create a diagnostic consensus among practitioners and encourage a diagnostic practice leading to greater reliability and validity. We feel that the implementation of DSM-III is desirable not only to promote accurate decisions concerning diagnosis, treatment, and management of children with psychiatric disorders, but also to foster dialogue within the profession and continued research efforts.

Within this manual, commentary is given on the manifestation of disorders, differentiation among syndromes, and quality of characteristics, along with descriptive case material illustrating clinical symptoms. Troublesome areas are indicated, with the hope that increased clinical awareness and record keeping will lead to more accurate classification in the future. The multiaxial approach of DSM-III is highlighted as a means of assessing the child from a variety of perspectives. It focuses on the exogenous factors influencing development, sources of disorder, as well as the child's limitations and capabilities.

DSM-III, as a phenomenological model, will require major changes and minor adjustments. The user must strive for an objective attitude toward diagnosis, realizing the benefits of conscientiously applying diagnostic guidelines without slavish adherence to every detail. In many instances, seemingly clear, precise descriptions of behavior call for judgments that are difficult and subjective. The diagnostic system is a tool that is useful when used with care and with a mind toward further improvement. It may be that DSM-IV will stipulate laboratory measures as validation of, or even as criteria for, certain diagnoses. If that were to happen, there would be drastic revisions in the grouping of disorders. Enlightened application of the principles of DSM-III will certainly influence the future of psychiatric diagnosis.

An Overview of Psychiatric Diagnosis in Pediatric Age Groups

Chapter 1

Historical Perspective on Diagnosis of Childhood Disorders

Child psychiatry is a very recent addition to scientific efforts to help persons with mental disorder. Around the turn of the century, Binet introduced the first psychometric measure for children but the scale was not used in this country until after 1910. This occurrence was closely followed by the application of psychoanalytic theory, which strongly influenced child psychiatry in that it viewed childhood experience as a determinant of adult psychopathology. The emphasis placed on the meaning of childhood events and their influence on later psychiatric disturbance evoked interest in obtaining information directly from children.

Dr. Leo Kanner's textbook, *Child Psychiatry* (Kanner, 1935), was a major milestone for American child psychiatry, marking its birth as a specialty in this country. Dr. Kanner's expositions served as a model of descriptive clarity and increased awareness and interest in the types of children depicted. His description of infantile autism is a well-known example. Dr. Kanner's text still provides one of the clearest examples for diagnosis in child psychiatry; in fact, in several categories DSM-III has little to add.

During the past 50 years, there has been an explosion of information describing human behavior at all ages, documenting developmental changes, and explaining mechanisms and processes of change. Although

5

child psychologists have formulated assessment techniques and have designed tests in a variety of cognitive and behavioral areas, impact upon research techniques has remained minimal except in the area of psychometric testing.

Perhaps the two most important influences upon modern diagnosis and measurement in child psychiatry have been the areas of psychopharmacology in this country and psychiatric epidemiology in Great Britain. The contribution of the Isle of Wight study (Rutter et al., 1970) cannot be overstated. Among other findings are the relative frequency of behavioral disturbance in childhood (over 6%), the powerful nonspecific association between neurologic illness and behavioral disorders, and the association of specific developmental disability with conduct disorder. This work remains a major influence on current research in the field.

During the 1950s psychopharmacology brought about dramatic changes in patient care and the direction of research and assessment in general psychiatry in this country and in Europe. The advent of rating scales, double blind techniques, and the new attention diagnosis received as a predictor for treatment outcome were the result of renewed interest in descriptive change in symptoms once effective treatments were available.

Pediatric psychopharmacology took considerably longer to get started, despite early reports of the efficacy of stimulants for treatment of behavioral disorders in children (Bradley, 1937) and general interest in child development in the 1930s and '40s. The use of rating scales to record initial symptom levels and subsequent changes has had a potent effect on present day clinical descriptions and ratings. It is not surprising that two recent textbooks on pediatric psychopharmacology (Weiner, 1977; Werry, 1978) emphasize the importance of measurement and diagnosis. The goal of physiological dissection of syndromes on the basis of drug response (though not particularly realized in child psychiatry, but an excellent heuristic principle) has led to careful delineation of syndromes among children participating in drug research trials.

Although in its early stages psychopharmacological research sparked acute interest in childhood diagnosis, the intrinsically practical question became whether or not the same medication works for similar or different indications. Thus, differences between Autism and Schizophrenia, or between Attention Deficit Disorder and Conduct Disorder, serve the practical benefit of helping predict possible treatment choice and outcome. It is no accident that about half of the DSM-III committee on disorders of childhood and adolescence consisted of researchers who were working in pediatric psychopharmacology.

Perhaps it is ironic that stimulant medications, which have a diagnostically nonspecific effect, comprise the single most influential group of compounds encouraging accurate clinical description in modern child psychiatry research. The very speed and reliability of the effects of such medications have inspired numerous junior clinicians and researchers to document their influence in a simple, objective fashion.

Much effort has gone into validating rating scales and exploring interview parameters which might predict or reflect stimulant drug effects. Recent research has shown that virtually all children will become less restless and more attentive when given a stimulant drug, and that clinical efficacy depends upon the individual. The optimism engendered by such demonstrated changes has had a profound effect. Perhaps simple, practical measurements, such as motor activity, have helped renew interest and faith in descriptive measures. Recent work with antidepressants has produced equally valid and reliable measures of change in depression, even in young children.

Diagnosis is vital for child psychiatry, and the natural history of this subspecialty makes propitious the timing of DSM-III for general as well as research use.

Chapter 2

Definition of Disorder

Classification is essential for scientific progress in any discipline. This is difficult enough in general psychiatry, but there are several added difficulties in child psychiatry which make the diagnostic process particularly challenging. To begin with, there is great lack of information about natural history, familial patterns, and developmental aspects of most of the childhood behavioral disorders. Because of this, most diagnostic categories have been generated on the basis of what clinicians agree they recognize from clinical description as fitting what they see in their own practice. The particular group of children seen and the type of clinic to which they go may vary widely among clinicians and introduce a referral bias, which means that clinicians' knowledge of disorders is limited by their experience.

Furthermore, there is wide variation in the degree to which child clinicians have been trained to be descriptive. Inferential recounting of a patient's difficulties is based on the quality of interaction with the child and his/her family or his/her extrapolations from fantasy. In terms of descriptive methods, general psychiatry is much further advanced than child psychiatry in having available standardized interview techniques and widely used rating scales (such as the Hamilton Scale for Depression). There are several such tools being generated for child psychiatry, but they are in the early stages of development and their effectiveness will depend on clear, descriptive communication and the ability to use multiple informants.

PROBLEMS IN ASSESSMENT

Assessing Informants

Very few children, particularly those under age 15, are likely to be self-referred. Therefore, presenting complaints will usually be from parents, school, community, or other professionals who may have seen the child in some special testing capacity. The result of this complexity is that the clinician must, at some level, simultaneously evaluate the sources of referral. Agreement among other sources, the interviewer, and interview data, particularly with young children, is often minimal or only for obvious behaviors (Stephens et al., 1980).

Another factor to keep in mind when evaluating the information obtained from multiple informants is the amount of time each informant is exposed to the child. Time of day and situation often vary widely and can influence the reliability of the informant's report.

In periods of social, family, and educational turmoil, the diagnostician must be alert to the possibility of referral bias and of weakness in the child's support system. Carried to extremes, this point of view undermines the diagnostic system; however, the point being presented here is simply that the child diagnostician must regularly consider whether or not an external limitation, for example a particular school system, is handicapping the child. Similarly, there are unhealthy family situations in which a child cannot be supported and no specific diagnosis should be given the child. The focus of typical child guidance "cases" can also shift when a family support system changes, such as when a parent remarries or divorces, when a child is born, or when a family moves away from an important caretaker. These types of events can and do influence the adult patient, and it seems only reasonable to give special consideration to similar stressors with pediatric patients.

The complexity is further compounded by the fact that weak support systems typically occur together with deviant behavior in the child, not instead of it. The V Code in DSM-III is for situations *not* attributable to mental disorder and specifically addresses this problem with a list of codes from which to choose the one best describing the situation. When a mental disorder *is* found in the child, Axis IV can be used to specify social stresses that may be contributing to the child's difficulties. The V Codes are described in detail in a later section.

Poor Self-Report Skills

The child's ability to communicate with the examiner can be limited by his age, language development, and conceptual ability. This is a particular concern when assessing expression of mood in young children. It is also difficult to obtain reports of motor restlessness, bizarre behavior, etc., directly from the child.

VALIDITY AND RELIABILITY OF DSM-III DIAGNOSES FOR CHILDHOOD DISORDERS

Validity of Axis I Diagnoses

DSM-III presents a mixture of "tried and true" diagnostic concepts, together with disorders that are extremely controversial. Included are many new categories that have been developed in order to provide a more explicit description of each patient.

Both the newness of the field of child psychiatry and the lack of systematic research have left the area with more ideas than validating studies. Thus, there is good agreement on the diagnosis of Conduct Disorder and fairly good agreement on the diagnosis of Infantile Autism; however, considerable controversy arises over whether or not Avoidant Disorder really belongs under other categories or in the nomenclature at all. Similarly, there has been continued opposition to Oppositional Disorder! The criteria for this disorder resemble most normal children at some time or other and only further studies will decide if this is a helpful category. The diagnosis of Identity Disorder has evoked criticism. Proponents feel that this disorder is unique to adolescence and may be self-limited. Opponents point to evidence that the adolescent period does not need special consideration when making differential diagnosis from Depression or Schizophrenia, and that "identity crises" often become those major psychiatric disorders.

The dilemma posed by these childhood conditions is that the very lack of research makes for relatively less validating data than for comparable diagnoses in general psychiatry. Although a more conservative approach would have been justified, the main benefit of the specificity of DSM-III is that careful follow-up of individually coded cases will help determine which codings are eliminated from DSM-IV. It may be that relatively rare conditions need not each have a specific and separate coding, unless there is evidence that outcome, etiology, response to treatment, etc., have important clinical distinctions. It is truly a great strength that a system contains the flexibility to allow needed omission, substitutions, and other changes; the scientific basis of our diagnostic system demands that specific, careful descriptions be made and that further scrutiny be applied to justify continuation of many of these categories.

Reliability of Axis I Diagnoses
The beginner to DSM-III may be overwhelmed at first by the operational definitions and the number of new diagnostic categories on Axis I. The specificity of the categories has made some feel that diagnosis will be difficult because too many patients will elude classification after all criteria are applied. Concern in other cases has been that if categories are too broad the patient will meet criteria but the diagnosis will not be clinically appropriate. In fact, a recent study suggests that problems using DSM-III indeed focus on Axis I, but that the major problem is differential diagnosis, rather than the anticipated struggle with detailed criteria. DSM-III is not designed to provide a diagnosis for every child; however, in the study mentioned previously (Cantwell, Russell, Mattison, & Will, 1979a, b), surprisingly few of the 24 cases were considered undiagnosable using DSM-III, and raters preferred DSM-III to DSM-II for each diagnosis.

This is not to say that no problems exist! As Cantwell et al. (1979a, b) found, certain cases and categories presented difficulty because of their ambiguity. Also, some obstacles to good reliability of diagnosis on Axis I have been identified. For example, adolescent emancipation problems, commonly seen by practitioners, have no satisfactory V coding. Adjustment Disorder may not be sufficiently well operationalized, and newer categories such as Separation Anxiety Disorder may be too unfamiliar to be sufficiently used.

The novelty of the multiaxial feature may cause confusion, thus affecting reliable diagnosis. Practitioners familiar with DSM-II will not be used to leaving Axis I blank and may feel constrained to make a diagnosis when none is expected. These specific features will be discussed under the separate disorders later in this guide.

Interrater Reliability
If two clinicians cannot agree that a particular set of symptoms is present, then the disorder will not be studied well enough to define its course, response to treatment, background features, etc., in order to decide whether or not it is a valid syndrome. Although there are undoubtedly Axis I diagnoses of unproven validity, no diagnoses are thought to be unreliable. The presence of these disorders as descriptive entities on Axis I indicates, at the very least, that clinicians in some numbers and with some authority felt that the clinical picture of each disorder appeared in sufficient

numbers of patients and represented a diagnostic entity in the form described. Furthermore, it is assumed that the entity can be communicated with sufficient clarity if agreement between two raters is achieved once the descriptors are stated. This certainly seems to be the case for broad categories. That is, users of DSM-III are likely to agree that a disorder is, for example, in the broad band of conduct disorder vs. attention deficit rather than depression vs. anxiety. However, the studies cited above and others (Rutter et al., 1979) have shown that disagreement within the broad categories is much more common. Some critics have felt that DSM-III has gone overboard with finer separations than can be reliably made, particularly within anxiety and "depressive" disorders.

The only formal study comparing interrater reliability on DSM-II and Axis I of DSM-III (Mattison, Cantwell, Russell, & Will, 1979) indicates very similar degrees of reliability between the two systems. There tends to be good agreement for cases of psychosis, conduct disorder, hyperactivity, and mental retardation, with considerably more disagreement for anxiety disorders. Despite its apparent complexity, there is as good or slightly better probability that two raters will agree using the DSM-III system, as compared to DSM-II. Within the wide spectrum, different subtypes of Anxiety Disorders, Depression, and Conduct Disorder may be hard to distinguish; however, it is the aim of DSM-III to help make this differentiation.

Chapter 3

Specific Diagnostic Issues for Child Clinicians

AGE-SPECIFIC MANIFESTATION OF DISORDER

Childhood disorders are uniquely characterized by developmental considerations that are central to many of the diagnostic entities. For example, enuresis would not be diagnosed as pathological at age five or six but would be at age 12. Similarly, characteristics of many two-year-olds, such as obstinacy or resistance to change, would be considered pathological symptoms if they still persisted at age five or six, whereas in an earlier period they are considered part of a normal developmental stage. Numerous examples can be cited and all raise interesting questions about where normal development stops and pathology begins. Separation anxiety is usual between eight months and two years of age, although this may not be universally true. It is not considered a pathological process, however, until ages three or four.

Diagnosis in Preschool Children

A central concern is whether or not any reliable and valid diagnosis can be made for preschool-aged children. A few follow-up studies support the predictive validity of diagnosis in young children (Wolff, 1961); however, psychiatrists are reluctant to utilize diagnoses at this age. Earls's recent study (1982) suggests that DSM-III diagnoses may prove appropriate even for three-year-olds, which would support the comprehensiveness of the system. Other data (Stephens et al., 1980) have shown that some behaviors may be reliably assessed in diagnostic interviews in this age group.

Adolescence as a Developmental Stage

The subject becomes even more complex when considering the later developmental stages. Considerable debate has ensued, for example, over the degree to which adolescence constitutes a special stage requiring singular diagnostic attention. For example, a DSM-III category which has no DSM-II counterpart is Identity Disorder. Much has been written about identity problems in adolescence, and college health services often make use of this category. While the strongest support for this subgroup has come from university health centers, these clinics often do not have long-term contact with the patients they treat and cannot provide additional information concerning outcome. Follow-up studies of adult disorders tend to argue for continuity over time when studying a specific diagnostic group (Welner, Welner, & Fishman, 1979). Such studies must be pursued in order to know if adolescent problems constitute a specific disorder (i.e., Identity Disorder) or predict adult pathology.

The decision was made to go ahead and include Identity Disorder as a category in DSM-III, even though there was insufficient systematically described, long-term follow-up information available. It may be that ultimately a substantial proportion of patients described by this disorder will be considered to have affective or schizophrenic disturbances, as has been the case for adolescent inpatients.

Like many diagnostic matters in child psychiatry, this is an area that produces strong opinion but suffers from a scarcity of facts. The virtue of DSM-III is that it provides clear description and definition of the disorder so that follow-up, family, and treatment studies can be carried out. Those results will decide the validity of the diagnostic distinctiveness of this condition.

REACTIVE NATURE OF CHILDHOOD DISORDERS

The Question of Family Diagnosis

Another issue raised when making diagnostic decisions about children is that of family diagnosis. During the meetings of the DSM-III Task Force Committee on Childhood Disorders, strong argument was put forth, particularly from the family therapists, that psychiatric diagnosis must go past its focus on the individual patient. Family work has identified types of families and family processes that, if ignored, could lead to artificial labeling of the child as a patient. This argument is particularly compelling in instances where change has occurred in the family structure and behavior problems have originated at that time, as when a child becomes a victim of marital discord. There are a number of less obvious clinical situations in which the nature of the interactions within the family unit may seem the most salient aspect of the case. Family therapists point out that family diagnosis is, in their experience, the most useful treatment prescription and predictor of treatment response that can be made.

While the importance of these arguments is not disputed, there is as yet no consensus or validation of information about specific family diagnoses. The V Codes in DSM-III can be useful for child psychiatrists in dealing with this issue at present. For example, V61.20 Parent-Child Problem or V61.80 Other Specified Family Circumstances can be used to indicate that the primary target is the family. These are to be used when the child has no diagnosed mental disorder or where the focus of treatment centers on family issues. Further goals for family therapists will be to identify reliable and valid family diagnostic entities, and to reach some consensus, so that these concepts can be incorporated into a diagnostic classification system.

Adjustment Disorder as a Diagnosis

The diagnosis of adjustment reaction and/or reactive disorder is frequently used, and has been overused by child psychiatrists. Only one diagnostic entity of this nature is presently incorporated in the childhood and adolescent section of the DSM-III, that is, Reactive Attachment Disorder of Infancy. This is a well documented condition, perhaps the best validated of any of the infant diagnoses. It is anticipated, however, that in addition to using this specific disorder in the child and adolescent section, child psychiatrists will continue to make steady use of the 309. series of Adjustment Disorder.

Traditionally, child psychiatrists' use of the diagnosis of Adjustment Reaction has been excessive and the profession has been strongly criticized for negating diagnostic description altogether. During a recent "third-party review" of residential treatment centers, for example, it was found that children who had been residents of centers for several years were still carrying the diagnosis of Adjustment Reaction of Adolescence (John Bartko, Ph.D., personal communication). Reasons for overuse of the term may stem from a desire to protect the privacy of the child or to reflect an optimistic outlook for the child's future. The point is that the diagnosis was rendered useless for communicating descriptive information. The DSM-III definition seeks to limit the use of "reactive" to a three-month period and also requires that some description of behaviors be included. Thus, adjustment disorder with depressed mood is differentiated from adjustment disorder with disturbance of conduct. This key feature will permit follow-up to determine whether or not the diagnosis can indeed predict a different outcome from a diagnosis of depression or conduct disorder.

One of the primary strengths of DSM-III, if used properly, is that it contains necessary information for its own revision. Any clinician who records such diagnoses and has the means to reexamine the cases at a later point in time, through follow-up, etc., will be able to systematically check on the validity of some of his or her own diagnostic formulations. For example, do children diagnosed as adjustment disorder with disturbance of conduct have a different outcome from children diagnosed as conduct disordered or those having adjustment disorder with anxious mood? Clinics and hospitals will be in a position to carry out this type of study in an even more extensive fashion.

ROLE OF INTELLECTUAL FUNCTIONING IN MENTAL DISORDERS

The importance of intellectual functioning in school-aged children, as well as the indirect assessment of some mood and thought states, has led to wide use of psychological testing. It is used more extensively with children than in general psychiatry and is heavily relied on for diagnosis and treatment planning. Such evaluation is especially encouraged for children who have behavioral or academic difficulties in school, or for children with an early developmental lag.

The high association of psychiatric disorder with mental retardation, as well as the differing emphasis placed upon intellectual level by psychiatrists, has elicited a strong push to rate intellectual functioning on a separate axis. This would avoid the ambiguity now present in DSM-III, where it is an Axis I assessment. A version of the International Classification of Diseases, Ninth Edition (ICD-9) used in Great Britain, in fact includes a separate level for intellectual functioning and requires that all patients be coded on that axis.

The problem with having intelligence assessed as an Axis I function is that some clinicians may choose it as a major diagnosis while others may ignore it completely. In other ways, however, DSM-III has brought improvements to this category. For example, the section defining Borderline Mental Retardation (IQ 71–84) has been eliminated and has been placed under a V Code (V62.88). Also, the mild, moderate, and severe distinctions in Mental Retardation correspond to the IQ levels designated by the international system and its British version (see Table 1).

The reason for keeping intellectual functioning on Axis I for DSM-III was, in part, social. There was concern that the subjects for whom social adaptive functioning was normal would be stigmatized by having intellectual level applied to them systematically. The other view was that Mental Retardation as a clinical syndrome must involve some impairment in adaptive functioning. There are still reservations about this difference between DSM-III and the initial proposal for a separate axis. Research elsewhere has shown that a recurring cause for diagnostic confusion among clinicians is the tendency for some to regularly include Mental Retardation as a primary diagnosis while others omit it altogether. The child psychiatrist may omit the diagnosis because he/she feels it is diagnostically unimportant for the presenting problem or because he/she does not recognize the problem. Having Mental Retardation entered on a separate axis would avoid this difficulty, as all cases would be required to be coded. As it stands now, DSM-III urges multiple diagnosis in such cases, but this recommendation is probably not followed systematically. It is more likely to be followed if the axis is separate.

IMPORTANCE OF MULTIPLE DIAGNOSES

DSM-III has a number of new diagnostic groupings that either have no counterpart in DSM-II or were derived from the splitting of broad DSM-II categories. From this wide selection, DSM-III encourages one to make multiple diagnoses, except when a specific differential diagnosis is required, as is the case between schizophrenia and affective disorder. A special consideration with respect to child diagnosis must be stressed at this point.

In light of the relative lack of validating information regarding diagnostic categories for children, why add to the confusion by using multiple categories for the same child? An important potential benefit is that it will provide information on which to base later decisions concerning multiplicity of groups and in weeding out overlap that may already exist in such areas as Attention Deficit Disorder and Conduct Disorder. Oppositional Disorder presents another controversial illustration. If Oppositional Disorder is always diagnosed together with Attention Deficit Disorder, should the two categories be joined or one eliminated? It may be

TABLE I
Coding of Intellectual Functioning for DSM-III and ICD-9/U.K.

DSM-III		ICD-9/U.K.	
Axis I. Mental Retardation		Axis III. Intellectual Level	
Subtypes	IQ Levels	Coding	IQ Levels
317.0 Mild	50–70	0. Normal Variation	
318.0 Moderate	35–49	1. Mild (Moron, feeble-minded)	50–70
318.1 Severe	20–34	2. Moderate (Imbecile)	35–49
318.2 Profound	Below 20	3. Severe (Imbecile NOS)	20–34
319.0 Unspecified	(IQ level is presumed to be below 70 but individual is untestable)	4. Profound (Idiocy)	Below 20
		5. Unspecified (Mental deficiency or subnormality NOS)	
V CODE:		6. Intellectual level unknown (Not assessed)	
V62.89 Borderline Intellectual Functioning	71–84		
A fifth digit code is specified for the Axis I subtypes. 1 = Behavioral symptoms requiring treatment; 0 = Absence of additional behavioral symptoms. IQ measure is obtained from individually administered testing. A five-point error of measurement allows some flexibility in defining IQ level.		Based on standardized test scores with mean = 100 and a standard deviation = 15.	

found that Oppositional Disorder predicts a similar outcome when compared to follow-up results for mild forms of Conduct Disorder. If that is the case, the delineating structures will have to be scrutinized and modified in order to avoid such duplication.

The use of multiple axes is the primary force ensuring that multiple diagnoses and complementary characteristics are recorded. There is, however, considerable question as to the extent to which multiple Axis I diagnoses should play such a role. The concept of DSM-III implicit in this notion is that multiple diagnoses will lead to better categorization. ICD-9 is in fundamental disagreement with this position. Opponents of the DSM-III view think that multiple diagnoses beg the question and that crucial clinical decisions about salient features of a case would be (inadvertently) avoided. Despite the differences of opinion, multiple categories are of express importance for DSM-III because of the relative multiplicity of highly specific diagnoses.

While DSM-III urges multiple diagnoses and will influence clinicians to make more individual diagnoses than did DSM-II, critics are also concerned that important differential diagnoses will not be made because of such multiple recordings. This is not likely to be so. In the first place, mutually exclusive differential diagnoses are made among some Axis I disorders, for example, between the different Pervasive Developmental Disorders, and between Attention Deficit Disorder and Schizophrenia. Specific symptoms can be accounted for by more than one disorder, such as Attention Deficit Disorder *or* Schizophrenia, to account for hyperactivity, but the nature of the disorders will determine the diagnosis.

In other disorders, it will be evident that some diagnoses, at least descriptively, are mild forms of another. For example, one would not make the diagnosis of Conduct Disorder and Oppositional Disorder, or Identity Disorder and Borderline Personality Disorder.

These are areas, however, where diagnostic combinations will remain murky. In practice it will be difficult to diagnose both moderate Mental Retardation and a Specific Developmental Disorder, although both are specifically suggested as common associates in the DSM-III manual. Similarly, when IQ is less than 50, in our opinion, it is very difficult to support an independent diagnosis of Infantile Autism.

The greatest diagnostic confusion will be created by children who show signs of more than one disorder: the mixture of anxiety/depression with conduct disorder or hyperactivity, for example, will give rise to diagnostic debate. Here, by urging multiple codings, DSM-III departs from both DSM-II and ICD-9, which would choose the salient disorder or else specifically code (312.3) "Mixed disturbance of emotions and conduct." Studies already show, however, that a multiaxial system goes a long way toward eliminating some of the confusion created by frequently associated disorders (Russell, Cantwell, & Mattison, 1979; Rutter et al., 1975; Stephens et al., 1980).

Basic Concepts for Pediatric Psychiatric Diagnosis

Chapter 4

The Purpose of Axis II

In addition to Axis I diagnoses for the pediatric age group, there are several other areas which comprise and complement the diagnostic evaluation. These derive from the comprehensive nature of the multiaxial system of the DSM-III and from issues related to collection of clinical information and the resulting implications for treatment. These underlying notions form an important framework within the diagnostic process and, especially for child psychiatry, will influence the direction of future study and knowledge.

The evolution of the multiaxial system of the DSM-III has been a milestone in psychiatry's quest for descriptive clarity. An axial system of diagnosis has been in use for the last 20 years within psychiatry, and child psychiatrists have been its strongest proponents (Rutter, Shaffer, & Shepherd, 1975). Discrepancies in diagnosis have previously occurred because clinicians chose to concentrate on one aspect of a child's problem while ignoring the presence of others or judging them insignificant to the presenting problem.

The Axis II designation for adult diagnoses is used for personality disorders; however, a special use of Axis II has been designated when diagnosing children and adolescents. It is designed to ensure that developmental disorders, such as reading and language disorders, are always recorded. When they are highlighted on a separate axis, their importance is not overlooked in future treatment planning and some conformity is provided within clinical practice for coding their presence.

SPECIFIC DEVELOPMENTAL DISORDERS

The separate axis notation of Specific Developmental Disorders is made even when psychiatric disorder is absent on Axis I. Multiple coding permits examination of the frequency and type of Specific Developmental Disorders associated with Axis I disorders. There is already evidence of specific associations between developmental disorders and some Axis I diagnoses—for example, the well-known affiliation between Conduct Disorder and Reading Disorder and at least nonspecific associations between speech and language delays and several Axis I disorders. The extent to which other specific disorders are connected to particular psychiatric syndromes is less clear.

Although controversy has surrounded the decision to include some of the developmental disorders as diagnoses of mental disorder, it is recognized that impairment of function and resulting distress are usually features of severe developmental disorder. In our opinion, a more serious flaw is that Axis II does not include a code for intellectual functioning. This may be a critical problem, since Mental Retardation is an Axis I diagnosis and may not get coded with sufficient frequency to obtain complete and accurate descriptions of different populations. This points out once again the importance of multiple diagnosis for Axis I disorders and emphasizes the need for thorough recording of Axis II Developmental Disorders and level of intellectual functioning within the child patient group.

PERVASIVE VS. SPECIFIC DEVELOPMENTAL DISORDERS

All disorders considered to be developmental in nature are characterized by disturbances in the initial development of basic functions. DSM-III provides a separate Axis I code for Pervasive Developmental Disorders, which should be distinguished from Axis II Specific Developmental Disorders. In Specific Developmental Disorders, functions of speech and language, reading, and arithmetic are specifically and selectively deficient. For Pervasive Developmental Disorders, severe distortions of functioning spread over many areas: social skills, language, attention, etc. The three categories within this set of disorders include Infantile Autism, which specifies that the disorder is apparent within the first 30 months of life; Childhood Onset; and Atypical. The latter two groups are of great research interest and must be carefully delineated, at least phenomenologically, from Infantile Autism to facilitate future study. There is, for example, speculation that the latter groups are closely related to schizophrenia; however, until biological or other measures are derived which will validate these separate categories, the descriptive approach of DSM-III seems the best available.

UNRESOLVED ISSUES

Status of Intellectual Level
There is general agreement among critics of DSM-III that level of intellectual functioning should be coded on a separate axis. In ICD-9, the international classification system as used in Great Britain, intellectual functioning is coded on a separate axis. Besides Axis I coding of Mental Retardation, the only other option for making any official notation of intellectual functioning is the V Code 62.88 (Borderline Intellectual Functioning). Since borderline intellectual functioning has not disappeared, this coding may be important for treatment planning or diagnosis when IQ is in the 71–84 range. A common clinical example is the child, without specific developmental disorder, who is identified as a "problem" in an academic environment. Evaluation reveals a relative intellectual impairment in a setting where range of achievement is slightly above average. This scenario is typical in many middle-class areas. The V Code 62.88 may be useful and should be used in such a situation. There are a host of social and philosophical issues concerning the merits of this label that cannot be dealt with in this context.

Enuresis and Encopresis as Developmental Disorders
In the early stages of DSM-III enuresis and encopresis were considered candidates for Axis II, along with other specific developmental disorders. One of the reasons for deciding not to include them was that a certain percentage of children with these disorders suffer from secondary, rather than primary, enuresis or encopresis. These children achieve voluntary bladder and bowel control, but then regress after toilet training is completed. This meant that secondary enuresis, for example, would be placed on Axis I while primary enuresis would go to Axis II. Having the same disorder on both Axis I and II seemed impractical. On Axis I, the distinction between primary and secondary conditions should be stressed as a matter of diagnostic significance, particularly for encopresis and to some extent enuresis. Although the inclusion of primary enuresis or encopresis as a "mental disorder" is objectionable, these disorders should be noted be-

cause of their frequent, although not invariable, association with behavioral disturbance. Nevertheless, regular occurrence as an isolated symptom and the tendency for higher frequency among males make primary enuresis much like other specific developmental disabilities. There may be cases where enuresis is the sole presenting complaint and, in the absence of associated behavioral disturbance, the diagnosis of the developmental disorder would have seemed more appropriate.

Chapter 5

The Use of Axes III, IV, and V in Pediatric Diagnosis

AXIS III. PHYSICAL DISORDERS AND CONDITIONS

The coding of medical or physical conditions on Axis III is a major part of the diagnostic formulation but will not be discussed here. These conditions correspond to those specified in ICD-9-CM. It is important, however, for the clinician to be aware of the major new insights that epidemiology has given child psychiatry in relation to Axis III disorders. For example, the Isle of Wight survey (Rutter et al., 1970) showed a powerful association between *all* neurological disorders and *all* behavioral syndromes, even though the association was completely nonspecific. If significant conditions exist, Axis III will be important for the understanding and management of a case.

Although the official diagnostic assessment is formulated on Axes I–III, Axes IV and V code supplemental information.

AXIS IV. SEVERITY OF PSYCHOSOCIAL STRESSORS

Axis IV, which deals with psychosocial stressors, is particularly helpful to child psychiatrists, in addition to whatever information is collected in specific clinical and research settings, since child clinicians have been keenly aware of the importance of environmental supports for normal development and the significance of stress in abnormal development.

Severity of psychosocial stressors, Axis IV, is determined by assessing quality, character, and quantity of events within the previous year, and addresses the importance of situational stress and support in many childhood disorders. Such an evaluation can determine, to some degree, any significant relationship between type, severity, improvement, or exacerbation of Axis I disorders and social stress. A seven-point scale is used to indicate severity: 0 = unspecified, 1 = none, 2 = minimal, 3 = mild, 4 = moderate, 5 = severe, 6 = extreme, 7 = catastrophic. The clinician is asked to rate the stressor and not the patient's reaction to it. The judgment involves distinguishing the number and type of significant stressors and considering their summed effect. In the British multiaxial version of ICD-9, presence or absence of stressors and specific stressors are coded on Axis V—see Appendix I for comparison. Of the groups of stressors suggested in DSM-III, the following may be exemplary of distresses encountered in childhood years: discord between parents, separation of parents, death of a parent, illness of a parent, problems in school, problems with peers, move to new home, a personally threatening event, puberty, illness, hospitalization, accident, physical impairment (also coded on Axis III), physical or mental disturbance of parent, abusive behavior on part of parent, deprived environmental situation, lack of or inconsistent parenting, etc. See DSM-III (p. 27) for examples illustrating the application of these ratings in children and adolescents.

It is also suggested that each stressor be listed in parentheses after the rating in order of etiological significance. It is hoped that the appropriate use of this axis will eliminate overuse of "adjustment reaction," which has plagued child psychiatry for so long, by providing a place to note stressors without avoiding or distorting the description of the case.

In formulating DSM-III, there were many ways psychosocial stressors could have been coded. For some, the choice of "Severity of Psychosocial Stressors" as the content of Axis IV was a purely arbitrary decision. It is not clear on what basis the present scale was chosen or whether it is relevant to children. Adequate interrater reliability has been reported for Axis IV (Russell, Cantwell, Mattison, & Will, 1979); however, for research purposes, at least with children, there are probably more interesting aspects of psychosocial stressors to code. For instance, the nature of stress (loss, parenting, economic factors) and the factors mediating the stress could be addressed. The supports available to handle the stress, rather than severity of the stress, may be the most crucial variables.

AXIS V. HIGHEST LEVEL OF ADAPTIVE FUNCTIONING

Axis V measures the individual's highest level of functioning within the previous year. In several adult studies, there is considerable prognostic value from this measure, particularly with schizophrenia. This type of indicator has been less studied with children; even if positive results are indicated, difficulty may arise in that the highest level of functioning is defined within a one-year period and therefore may be confounded with the duration of the illness. The limitation of one year may mislead ratings for disorders continuing for more than one year.

It is also possible, however, that directing some attention on the part of the clinician to the strengths of the child may uncover information peculiar to the therapy of the individual child and also serve as an index of the child's functioning over time. DSM-III provides a table (pp. 29, 30) showing the use of the seven levels of functioning with examples for coding Axis V. Information is derived from three areas: social relations, particularly with family and peers; achievement as a student based on performance; and use of leisure time, which includes hobbies, sports, learned skills, and recreational activities.

Research focusing on the issues surrounding the contents of Axis IV and V is needed. Careful use of these axes can help to clarify the troubling dispute concerning "reactive disorder" and "adjustment reaction." By coding behavior on Axis I and social factors on Axis IV, the relative predictive usefulness of both or either can be compared by follow-up studies or observation of treatment response.

PROBLEMS OF MEASUREMENT IN PSYCHIATRIC EVALUATION

By now it must be obvious to the reader that diagnostic practices with children differ substantially from those used with adults. In most instances, the clinician is required to use numerous resources in order to obtain reliable information and make an accurate evaluation.

The Importance of Multiple Informants

As mentioned previously, the fact that a child does not initiate his or her own treatment affects the diagnostic process considerably. Parents may be worried that their child seems upset or unhappy or they may be distressed by the child's behavior. In either case the child may or may not be aware of the concern elicited in others and has little input in the procedures that bring him/her to the examiner.

The child psychiatrist must balance his/her assessment, weighing the sensitivity and perspective of the informants, most often the parents. Parents vary in their expectations, experience, and tolerance of children; they may also disagree between themselves about the child's difficulties. Other opinions and informants are extremely useful in constructing a comprehensive view of the child's situation. A teacher's perceptions are valuable for acquiring information concerning inattentive, hyperactive, or aggressive behavior. Additional reports from other relatives or even community members may be helpful in understanding the severity and situationality of the disturbance.

Psychological Testing
Psychological testing is more beneficial in diagnosing children than adults because of the strong association between intellectual functioning and many areas of behavioral disturbance. For instance, Mental Retardation and Specific Development Disorders usually require psychometric testing before the diagnosis can be made. The tester serves as an additional observer and can employ techniques for indirect measure of mood and behavior, especially important for children with poor self-report skills. Projective tests, however, are not particularly important for settling diagnostic questions (Gittelman, 1980).

Neurological
Examination
Neurological examination has a relatively small role in the process of diagnosing childhood disorders. Its primary use is to rule out neurological disorders; it does not add substantially to treatment planning. Various childhood disorders are, however, associated statistically with neurological correlates, such as motor clumsiness and overflow with specific developmental disabilities and behavioral disorders. Attention Deficit Disordered children are often described as having soft neurological signs or a mildly abnormal EEG.

Interview With the Child
The feasibility of semi-structured interviews for children, their thoroughness, and successful identification of homogeneous populations in research efforts suggest that such a tool is a useful addition to the routine clinical child psychiatric evaluation. Play interviews are used to assess preoccupations, conflicts, symbolic meanings, and psychodynamic constellations. For preschool children, this may be the only way to gain information in a reliable way (Stephens et al., 1980).

The interview with the child is particularly important in the diagnosis of Anxiety Disorders and Depression. In these areas the child, even the young child, is the best informant. Direct observation of behavior varies in significance when diagnosing other disorders, however. For example, a child with Attention Deficit Disorder, particularly an older child, may not manifest signs of inattentiveness and restlessness during the interview. Although play interviews may be essential in psychotherapy for establishing and maintaining a relationship, they should not be depended on to assess symptomatology, as they often will not identify symptoms like hallucinations, suicidal thoughts, or frequent obsessions. The use of some semi-structured interview with the child or adolescent is essential to making a psychiatric diagnosis.

Use of Rating Scales
Nowhere in DSM-III is it specified that rating scales are to be used in the diagnostic process; however, it seems desirable that every clinician become familiar with some of the common scales available for rating clinical severity and change. These scales provide a powerful means of communication across centers and furnish an efficient and economical way of following treatment patterns and predicting outcome. They can afford a base from which any clinic can establish systematic research. There has often been a negative reaction to the use of rating scales in private practice. Some clinicians are reluctant to use ratings for fear that they will detract from the more subtle clinical evaluation and establishment of rapport during the interview. This is seldom the case. In fact, many clinicians report that they are more free to explore other areas knowing that the presence and severity of symptoms have been carefully documented.

The choice of rating form will depend on the type of practice, the time available for completing it, and the informants used. The Conners parent and teacher scales and the Achenbach parent and teacher scale have proven very useful in numerous settings. The Conners rating scales have been successfully employed in the evaluation of drug trials as a means of tracking changes. As an initial neurological screening exam, the PANESS, or its abbreviated version, is helpful. Guidelines for the use and evaluation of these scales are readily available. (See Appendix II for listing of sources.) For more information on available scales and their uses, see Goldman, Stein, and Guerry (1984).

Changes Over Time
Although DSM-III is clearer and more specific than any previous diagnostic nomenclature, there are some instances when one must go it alone.

One problem is that some disorders change over time. In particular situations, it is extremely difficult to make an initial diagnosis; in other cases, the quality of the basic symptomatology has changed.

A case in point is the diagnosis of the developmental disorders. Infantile Autism, for example, is diagnosed when the symptoms have appeared during the first 30 months of life; however, reports of gross and sustained impairment of social relationships are difficult to interpret when the child is older and has gained some partial skills. A parent may claim that the child is relating; yet, the clinician may fail to detect any relating behaviors. Some children, through repeated association, appear to have formed superficial relationships, though far from normal. The clinician has little to go on in assessing this aspect of symptom quality except his/her own experience.

The manifestations of the specific developmental disorders vary considerably with stages of development and degree of disability. It is not always possible to diagnose speech and language disorders during the first three years of life, for this is the period when speech normally begins. Developmental reading disorders are not recognized until the first few years of school. Diagnosis should take these age levels into account; for example, if a child is clearly below age level on a reading readiness test, but still below an age when reading is expected, as frequently seen with kindergarten students, diagnosis should not be attempted at the time. At later ages, reading disability may still be apparent, though less pronounced. In fact, it is common for previously diagnosed adolescents and even adults to continue to show persistent signs of developmental reading disorder. In such cases, the disorder should still be coded, indicating its mild form, since there is no "residual state" code for these categories. Clinically, the boundaries between the different specific developmental disorders are often unclear. For instance, many children diagnosed as having speech and language disabilities gain normal speech but later have reading difficulties.

Specific criteria are not spelled out for each of the developmental disorders and it is up to the clinician to come up with his/her own formulation, even though there may be differences in definition of terms. For some, a significant delay in reading may be one year below grade level; for others, it must be two years. The specification of standardized and individually administered tests is of course helpful and necessary, but the clinician is left with more decisions to make for this particular category than for the other child sections in DSM-III.

Chapter 6

Treatment Strategies in Relation to Diagnosis

PATIENT AS CASE VS. DIAGNOSIS AS DISORDER

The diagnostic process answers the questions: "Is a psychiatric disorder present?" and "If so, does it fit a known clinical syndrome?" During this procedure a great amount of clinical information is generated that assists in understanding the individual case and planning treatment and management of the patient. When treating a child, it is crucial to gain knowledge of the familial, social, and biological roots of the problem, of the forces maintaining the problem and facilitating the child's development, and of the child's individual strengths.

If intervention is necessary, then the specific diagnosis is only one piece of the information needed in order to develop an appropriate treatment plan. A recommendation is made depending on the attitude of the family and child, the practitioner's own expertise and judgment, and, perhaps most important, information concerning the natural outcome of the disorder without treatment.

DSM-III AND DRUG TREATMENT:
THE MYTH OF "ONE DISORDER—ONE DRUG"

Management through medication is likely to be the most complex direction treatment planning can take, and the issues involved require careful scrutiny. Of primary importance when this type of program is considered, is whether or not medication is the right route to take with a particular child. An assessment needs to be made of the child's sense of helplessness, the significance of medication to the family and/or school, and the severity of condition—whether or not it improves spontaneously or deteriorates. These factors may influence the choice of a particular drug or argue against the use of any drug at all. In addition, information concerning drug response within specific diagnostic groups and evidence of familial influence on drug response may assist in the selection of medication. Although these latter areas are topics of research, the implications for individual application cannot be ignored. For example, individual hyperactive children may respond selectively to dextroamphetamine or methylphenidate. Treatment must be based on empirical data obtained on an individual basis. Two different clinical groups have shown preliminary evidence that a pattern of disorder within the family may influence drug response in offspring. In one study adolescents with positive history of Gilles de la Tourette's syndrome within the family were more likely to respond to haloperidol (Nee, Caine, Polinsky, Eldridge, & Ebert, 1980). Similar reports suggested that a history of lithium response in a parent was associated with a beneficial response to a lithium trial in children with a variety of behavioral and affective disturbances and problems with impulse control (Dyson & Barcai, 1970; McKnew, Cytryn, Buchsbaum, Hamovit, Lamour, Rapoport, & Gershon, 1981).

PHARMACOTHERAPY AND CHILDHOOD DISORDERS
Since pediatric psychopharmacology is still in its early stages, DSM-III will enable a systematic assessment of patients as part of research and provide the methodology to address questions concerning diagnosis and treatment. Until now, most work has primarily used a target approach, focusing on changes in individual symptoms, for example, stereotypy or classroom restlessness, in order to establish the efficacy of drug treatment. Little is known of the diagnostic specificity of drug effect and no relationship between drug and diagnosis has yet been established (Gittelman-Klein, Spitzer, & Cantwell, 1978). The information that has been collected thus far should stimulate further investigation of the relationship between DSM-III diagnostic categories and the choice of somatic treatment.

Mental Retardation
Limited work in pharmacotherapy of retarded children has focused on target behaviors such as stereotypy, self-abuse, impulse control, and hyperactivity (Sprague & Baxley, 1978); no data have been collected con-

cerning the influence of retardation per se on drug response. It is not known whether the degree of retardation influences the likelihood of drug response or the choice of drug. For example, phenothiazines may be more effective in treating hyperactivity in retarded individuals than in children with normal intelligence, but this has not been systematically studied. DSM-III only provides coding for the presence of behavioral disturbance in a retarded individual. Although Mental Retardation is frequently associated with other Axis I disorders such as Attention Deficit or Movement Disorders, in our opinion such additional coding should not be given when IQ is below 50. Presence of associated behavioral symptoms with Mental Retardation that require treatment should be indicated with the fifth digit code.

Attention Deficit Disorder
A major innovation of DSM-III has been the separation of Attention Deficit Disorder from Conduct and Oppositional Disorders. The benefits of stimulant drug treatment have been carefully documented in regard to restless, impulsive behavior. The prototype patient referred for stimulant drug treatment has a diagnosis of Attention Deficit Disorder. This reclassification has encouraged investigation of the benefit of stimulants for individuals with Conduct or Oppositional Disorder without Attention Deficit Disorder and leaves one to speculate whether or not Attention Deficit, Oppositional, and Conduct Disorders represent a continuum of impulsivity rather than separate diagnostic entities.

Stereotyped Movement Disorders
DSM-III permits specification of several types of movement disorder. It is only for Tourette's syndrome that response to haloperidol has been firmly established (Shapiro, Shapiro, & Wayne, 1973). A question of concern is whether haloperidol treatment is effective for a particular category of movement disorder. It may be that all chronic motor tics (without a verbal component) and other "atypical" tics also respond to haloperidol.

Pervasive Developmental Disorders
Considerable confusion with regard to drug treatment of these conditions has arisen in part from changes in diagnostic terminology (severe conditions were previously labeled Childhood Psychosis). Drug treatment remains an empirical and largely unsatisfactory approach to these disorders (Campbell, Geller, & Cohen, 1977). Phenothiazines, although not specifically useful for the primary deficit of these disorders (Gittelman-Klein et al., 1978), are somewhat effective in the treatment of common secondary

symptoms such as hyperactivity and aggressivity. Thus, while pharmacotherapy may prove a useful adjunct to treatment of the pervasive developmental disorders, drug choice must be based on a target symptom approach.

GENERAL GUIDELINES FOR TREATMENT MODALITIES

Assessment and identification of a disorder are only two parts of the diagnostic process. The formulation and continuing evaluation of a treatment plan are vital elements of this procedure. DSM-III, however, does not claim to be a cookbook of treatment recipes, and its less inferential framework in no way implies treatment preferences for specific disorders. Treatment issues are much more extensive than diagostic ones; yet that very fact inspires continued striving for clarity of description within diagnosis and research of treatment response in relation to disorder.

It is generally agreed that once a diagnosis is determined, all treatment decisions should first involve assessing the present severity and the probable outcome if the condition is untreated. Once the decision in favor of treatment is reached, timing becomes an important element; for example, if a situation appears to be resolving spontaneously, that may not be the time to recommend a new intervention.

Diagnostic and treatment issues may be conceptually different for many family therapists who feel that an appropriate diagnosis should be applied to the family as a whole rather than to the identified patient. This type of therapy investigates why the child has become the identified patient, and how the family can be changed in order to provide mutual support when dealing with current and future problems.

If behavioral therapy is considered, an analysis of problem behaviors is essential, and objective rating forms provide an excellent means for doing so. Observing the frequency of problem behaviors and the circumstances in which they occur leads to an understanding of how the negative behaviors were acquired, formulated, and maintained. Compliance with psychodynamically oriented treatments, as well as with behavior therapy, is heavily influenced by the motivation to receive treatment, the ability of the child and the family members to relate to the clinician, and the quality of the interaction among family members (O'Leary & Carr, 1982). The family's past experiences with psychiatric treatment and their attitude toward therapy will be major factors in determining the kind of treatment they will accept.

Focus on the Family

The importance of the family in the treatment of the child is self-evident, and family report is inextricably entwined in the diagnostic process. Many feel that family diagnostic interviewing is the most appropriate approach and should be the major tool of child practitioners. At this stage there is no validated diagnostic system that is generally accepted by family therapists. It is possible that the V Codes will be amplified in the future and then more formal categories of family pathology can be proposed. At present, when no Axis I disorder is apparent, V61.10 Marital Problem or V61.20 Parent-Child Problem can be used by therapists to indicate that the interaction between family members accounts for the presenting symptom, for example, sibling rivalry, a difficulty with another relative living in the household, etc. Until some other method is installed, the identification and recording of certain family attitudes remain a practical consideration. The clinician should in some way register those instances when parents bring a child for evaluation and it becomes apparent that the couple is seeking help for themselves. In such a case marital counseling becomes the most appropriate treatment and may not involve the child at all.

In summary, evaluation and treatment planning go far beyond identification of a disorder and the diagnostic process is much broader than recognizing DSM-III entities. It is hoped that future research will specify treatment response so that it can become a validating feature of some disorders, but at this time treatment response is one of the least helpful features in validating a disorder, even in the area of drug treatment. DSM-III in no way removes the burden of understanding the "case."

Major Classifications and Differential Diagnosis

Chapter 7

Classification of
Childhood Disorders
in DSM-III

The DSM-III classification system separates some 200 disorders into 18 diagnostic groupings. Of those, Disorders Usually First Evident in Infancy, Childhood, or Adolescence contains conditions which are frequently observed during the early period of life. Although these categories represent diagnostic situations typical of this age group, consideration of *all* DSM-III diagnoses is appropriate at any stage of life. In fact, initial investigation suggests that child psychiatrists are underutilizing many general categories when making childhood assessments because primary application of these diagnoses has been with adults. Common examples of "adult" diagnoses which can expect regular use are Schizophrenic Disorders, for children having a childhood onset of a thought disorder; Affective Disorder for the increasing number of children who are recognized as having Major Depressive Episodes, Single or Recurrent; and Substance Use Disorders, primarily for the adolescent population. At least two studies found that more than 20% of children and adolescents seen at academic child psychiatry clinics fit unmodified DSM-III criteria for Major Depressive Disorder (Puig-Antich, 1982; Carlson & Cantwell, 1982).

It is important to emphasize that the conditions clustered under the infant, childhood and adolescent heading are not the only diagnoses pertinent to this group, and that these disorders may also occur in adults. DSM-III rarely defines age boundaries, but in several instances age is specified within the diagnostic criteria and may be a key in differential diagnosis between child and adult disorders.

In the following chapters, major DSM-III classifications applicable to impaired functioning in the pediatric age group are compared with respect to diagnostic criteria and differential diagnosis. Despite emphasis on classification, one must keep in mind that observation and recognition, description and identification are important links in the diagnostic system. Classification organizes the observations by the descriptions; in DSM-III, specific diagnostic criteria and differential diagnosis are the organizing factors. In order to make a complete diagnosis, DSM-III provides additional information for each disorder concerning associated features, age at onset, course, impairment, complications, predisposing factors, prevalence, sex ratio, and familial pattern. The following comments on these disorders should help the clinician to use DSM-III for childhood diagnosis.

The format used in this section basically sticks to the organization of DSM-III's section on Disorders First Evident in Infancy, Childhood, or Adolescence. In some instances, where differential distinctions become cloudy, several disorders are discussed side by side. Also included are two general diagnostic categories, Schizophrenia and Affective Disorder, which present special problems for diagnosis within the pediatric population. Some diagnoses are straightforward enough in their application that discussion is limited to instances involving differential diagnosis.

TABLE 2
Other DSM-III Disorders That Can Be Applied
to Children and Adolescents

1. Organic Mental Disorders may occur at any age.
   a. Delirium is especially common in children.
   b. Dementia can occur at any age due to specific etiologic factors.
   c. Organic Personality Syndrome is recognized by significant changes in child's usual behavior patterns (instead of personality). In a situation where there is Attention Deficit Disorder (ADD) with organic etiology (i.e., known neurological disease) only ADD is diagnosed—not Organic Personality Syndrome—if the disturbance is limited to impairment of impulse control and attention (DSM-III, pp. 119, 120).
2. Substance Use Disorders
3. Schizophrenic Disorders. Onset usually during adolescence or early adulthood. See Chapter 10 on Schizophrenia.
4. Paranoid Disorders. These generally arise in middle or late adult life.

TABLE 2 *(continued)*

5. Psychotic Disorders Not Elsewhere Classified
   a. Brief reactive psychosis—usually appears in adolescence or early adulthood.
6. Affective Disorders
   a. Major depressive episode can occur at any age.
   b. Dysthymic disorder may begin in childhood or adolescence, but usually begins early in adult life. See Chapter 11 on Affective Disorders.
7. Anxiety Disorders
   a. Agoraphobia. Most frequent onset is in late teens or early twenties.
   b. Social Phobia often begins in late childhood or early adolescence.
   c. Simple Phobia. Age at onset varies. Animal phobias nearly always begin in childhood.
   d. Panic Disorder often begins in late adolescence or early adult life.
   e. Obsessive Compulsive Disorder may begin in childhood; usually begins in adolescence or early adulthood.
   d. Hypochondriasis commonly appears in adolescence.
8. Dissociative Disorders
   a. Psychogenic Amnesia is most often observed in adolescent and young adult females.
   b. Multiple Personality. Onset may be in early childhood but it is rarely diagnosed until adolescence.
   c. Depersonalization Disorder usually begins in adolescence.
9. Psychosexual Disorders
   a. Gender Identity Disorder of Childhood.
   b. Transsexualism. Full syndrome usually appears in late adolescence or early adulthood.
   c. Fetishism usually begins by adolescence.
   d. Exhibitionism may occur at any time from preadolescence to middle age.
   e. Ego-dystonic Homosexuality. Onset is usually during early adolescence.
10. Factitious Disorders
11. Disorders of Impulse Control Not Elsewhere Classified
   a. Pathological gambling usually begins in adolescence.
   b. Kleptomania. Onset may be as early as childhood.
   c. Pyromania. Onset is usually in childhood.
12. Adjustment Disorder may begin at any age. See section in Chapter 15 on Adjustment Disorder.
13. Psychological Factors Affecting Physical Condition
14. Personality Disorders (Axis II) are usually recognizable by adolescence or earlier and continue through most of adult life, but should not be coded unless stability of pattern can be assessed with certainty. See corresponding Axis I diagnostic categories for Disorders Usually First Evident in Infancy, Childhood, or Adolescence (Table 3).
15. V Codes*
   a. V61.20 Parent-child problem
   b. V62.30 Academic problem
   c. V61.80 Other specified family circumstances

(continued)

TABLE 2 *(continued)*

    d. V62.82 Uncomplicated bereavement
    e. V62.88 Borderline intellectual functioning
    f. V62.89 Phase of life problem or other life circumstance problem
    g. V71.02 Childhood or adolescent antisocial behavior
16. Additional Codes
    a. 300.90 Unspecified mental disorder (nonpsychotic)
    b. V71.09 No diagnosis or condition on Axis I
    c. 799.90 Diagnosis or condition deferred on Axis I
    d. V71.09 No diagnosis on Axis II
    e. 799.90 Diagnosis deferred on Axis II
Note: Generalized Anxiety Disorder and Antisocial Personality Disorder are never diagnosed under 18 years of age.

    *See Chapter 15 on V Codes.

Chapter 8

Diagnosis of Personality Disorders in Children

DSM-III makes an attempt to provide Axis I parallels for children and adolescents with Axis II adult personality disorders (see Table 3). If the symptoms diagnosed in childhood persist after age 18, then the diagnosis would change to the corresponding adult personality disorder. In some cases, this seems to be a logical progression; however, in the case of Oppositional Disorder and Identity Disorder some disagreement is bound to ensue.

TABLE 3
Axis I Disorders Usually First Evident in Infancy, Childhood, or Adolescence and Corresponding Axis II Disorders

Disorders of Childhood or Adolescence (Axis I)	Personality Disorders (Axis II)
*Schizoid Disorder of Childhood or Adolescence	Schizoid Personality Disorder
*Avoidant Disorder of Childhood or Adolescence	Avoidant Personality Disorder
Conduct Disorder	Antisocial Personality Disorder
Oppositional Disorder	Passive-Aggressive Personality Disorder
Identity Disorder	Borderline Personality Disorder

*If features continue after age 18 change diagnosis to appropriate Axis II personality disorder.

In general, most personality disorders may be diagnosed in children or adolescents, although there is less certainty at these ages that the personality disorder will persist over time. Antisocial Personality Disorder, however, is not diagnosed under age 18. Criteria for diagnosing personality disorders in children are outlined in Table 4.

TABLE 4
Summary of Age Criteria and Differential Criteria for Diagnosis of Personality Disorders in Children

1. 301.20 *Schizoid Personality Disorder*
   a. If under 18, does not meet criteria for Schizoid Disorder of Childhood or Adolescence.
   b. The diagnosis of Schizoid Disorder of Childhood or Adolescence preempts the diagnosis of Schizoid Personality Disorder until after age 18, at which time the diagnosis is changed.
2. 301.70 *Antisocial Personality Disorder* by definition begins before the age of 15 but such a diagnosis is *not* made in children and is reserved for adults over age 18 who show full longitudinal pattern.
3. 301.83 *Borderline Personality Disorder*
   a. If under 18 and does not meet criteria for Identity Disorder.
   b. Diagnosis of Identity Disorder preempts this diagnosis.
4. 301.82 *Avoidant Personality Disorder*
   a. Diagnosis of Avoidant Disorder of Childhood or Adolescence preempts this diagnosis if under 18.
   b. If under 18 and does not meet criteria for Avoidant Disorder of Childhood or Adolescence.
5. 301.60 *Dependent Personality Disorder.* Anxiety Disorder and Avoidant Disorder of Childhood or Adolescence should be considered first. Chronic physical illness may predispose the development of this disorder in children or adolescents.
6. 301.84 *Passive-Aggressive Personality Disorder.* Oppositional Disorder preempts this diagnosis if under 18; however, if patient is under 18 and does not meet criteria for Oppositional Disorder, this diagnosis may be given.

Chapter 9

Developmental Abnormalities in the First Years of Life

Pervasive Developmental Disorder is used to describe the occurrence of extreme developmental abnormalities that are not normal for any stage of development and represent a distortion in development. Developmental impairment pervades areas of language, social skills, intellectual functioning, and emotional development. Basic psychological functions such as attention, perception, reality-testing, and motor movement are affected at the same time and to a severe degree. DSM-III avoids classifying these disturbances in the same manner as adult psychosis because of marked differences in the qualitative nature of psychotic disorders.

There are three subclasses of disorders in this category: Infantile Autism, Childhood Onset, and Atypical. With the possible exclusion of autism, a clear syndromal picture is hard to secure and may cause difficulties for differential diagnosis. In autism, diagnosis relies heavily on reports of early behavior, usually provided by the parent. In older Pervasive Developmentally Disordered (PDD) children, it may be difficult to elicit a clear retrospective description of early infant behavior. In both instances, parental bias may confuse the issue. The most commonly associated Axis I diagnosis is Mental Retardation. Diagnostic differentiation between subclasses of PDD is desirable for research concerning the nature of pathology or issues of prognosis, but is not necessary for clinical management.

Pervasive Developmental Disorders are extremely incapacitating and almost always require special educational facilities. Drug management with antipsychotics has little effect on core features but helps control secondary symptoms such as hyperactivity, excitability, moodiness, destructiveness, and sleeplessness. This type of treatment may allow continued home care by assisting parents in behavioral management; however, if no gains are apparent, continued administration seems of little clinical value. Behavior modification programs may offer a degree of behavioral control, but require rigorous enforcement on the part of parents and are likely to be ineffective outside a therapeutic setting.

The chronic nature of PDD requires long-term treatment and therapeutic goals should be directed toward specialized educational programs that may facilitate a degree of self-care and social functioning. Drug treatment is recommended only if it provides a reasonable level of improvement.

FOCUS ON AUTISM

Infantile Autism has not been included as a separate category in previous diagnostic manuals of the American Psychiatric Association, although various sets of diagnostic criteria have been defined elsewhere (Creak, 1964; GAP, 1974; Kanner, 1935; Ornitz & Ritvo, 1976). DSM-III has separated the category from its earlier association with psychosis and classified it as a developmental disorder, emphasizing the distortion of skills and functions which are normally acquired within the first 30 months of life. These distortions include three areas: social nonresponsiveness, impaired or peculiar language, and bizarre responses to various aspects of the environment.

Lack of Social Responsiveness

Autism, broadly defined, primarily describes an extreme social indifference and lack of responsivity. This emphasis is maintained in the DSM-III criteria, although clinicians may differ in judgment on the quality of such social nonresponsiveness, especially since onset of symptoms before 30 months of age is a diagnostic criterion. As outlined by DSM-III, this feature includes a lack of reaction to or interest in people to the extent that normal attachment behavior does not occur. A problem for clinicians to consider is that retrospective diagnosis of older children may confuse superficial sociability with apparent social relatedness.

Infant and childhood nonresponsiveness can be manifested in the following ways:

- failure to cuddle
- lack of eye contact
- lack of facial expression
- indifference or aversion to affection
- indifference or aversion to physical contact
- adults treated as interchangeable
- mechanical clinging to a specific adult
- failure to develop cooperative play
- failure to develop friendships

Older children may attain a level of superficial sociability, such as:

- awareness of parents or familiar adults
- attachment to parents or familiar adults only, but failure to relate to others
- passive involvement in games or physical play

These abnormal social behaviors also tend to vary with age and the severity of the illness, although the deficit is exacerbated during interactions requiring initiative or reciprocal behaviors. While the child may not withdraw from physical interactions such as rough-housing or tackling, he is unable to engage in imaginative play or participate in cooperative play. Whether or not this abnormality is a primary or secondary defect, it certainly is a pronounced feature. Autistic adolescents and adults continue to exhibit skill deficits and social inappropriateness in personal interactions.

Impaired Ability to Communicate

Both verbal and nonverbal areas of communication may be affected, and ability seems to vary according to stage of development and severity of the disorder. Language impairments can be evidenced in the degree of language development or in peculiar patterns of speech such as echolalia or the use of neologisms. Language may be immature and minimal, lacking in spontaneity, or, in the higher functioning patient, may be characterized by concreteness and nominal aphasia. Repetitive speech is also common, as is pronominal reversal and inability to use abstraction or metaphor. Some patients can readily decode written material, but show impairments in reading and comprehension. Nonverbal avenues of communication—gestures, facial expressions, and posture—are rarely used to compensate for impaired language abilities.

Bizarre Responses to Environment
Another characteristic which forms a larger part of the behavioral repertoire of the autistic child is his or her unusual and often bizarre responses to aspects of the environment. These may be evident in ritualistic or compulsive behaviors, attachments to certain objects, or extreme negative reactions to changes. This phenomenon has been explained as an adaptive response that is elicited because the child is unable to flexibly adapt to modifications in the environment and attempts to preserve what is known. Such reactions tend to diminish with age, though they rarely disappear and may become more complex or organized.

Absence of Psychotic Features
The symptoms apparent in schizophrenia, such as delusions, hallucinations, loosening of associations, and incoherence, are excluded from the diagnosis of autism. DSM-III has tried very hard to separate the former concept of childhood psychosis from the diagnosis of autism. It is difficult, in any case, to make an accurate assessment of the presence or absence of these kind of symptoms in language-impaired or nonverbal children.

Secondary Characteristics
Other characteristics, though not specific to autism, are often included in the description of the syndrome. These include lability, sensory responsiveness, and self-injury. Rocking and other rhythmic body movements also occur.

Diagnostic Issues
Evidence of relatedness. When there is evidence of relatedness at some point, an issue that may occur when making a retrospective diagnosis, can a diagnosis of autism be made? Unless a reliable history is available, can autism be diagnosed in an older child? Because symptoms change over time, this disorder becomes increasingly difficult to diagnose once the child is past age five. Parents, as informants, may be retrospectively biased and tend to report current assessments based on what the

child was like when younger. In these instances, the clinician must make his/her own judgments. For example, an ability to use facial expression to send and receive messages, to use gestural communications, to establish eye contact, or to demonstrate non-passive participation in play would indicate a minimal degree of relatedness. Unrelatedness would seem to require an inability both to use complex nonverbal communication and to exhibit an anhedonic quality of affect.

Though DSM-III provides specific guidelines for this disorder, subjective assessments must still be used to quantify the pervasiveness of diagnostic features.

Mental Retardation: Differential diagnosis. DSM-III states that if both disorders are present, two Axis I diagnoses should be made. In Mental Retardation, behavioral abnormalities similar to autistic symptoms are sometimes apparent. The full syndrome of Infantile Autism, however, is rarely present in Moderate Mental Retardation and would seem difficult to diagnose in severely or profoundly retarded individuals.

A recommendation for future classification would be to add an IQ criterion to the diagnosis for autism, with provision for the assessment of nonverbal children with a standardized nonverbal measure. Best estimates indicate that only 40% of children with autism have IQ scores of less than 50. Extreme variability in intellectual functioning has been demonstrated within this diagnostic group. Other studies indicate that performance tends to be characteristically low for symbolic or abstract thought, while it may be good for manipulative or visuo-spatial skills or rote memory. The presence of one or more areas of normal intellectual ability, despite subtest scatter, could also be added to the criteria.

Coding

Associated physical disorders. Associated physical disorders should be coded on Axis III. Maternal rubella seems to be the most common. Epileptic seizures have been reported to develop in adolescence or adulthood in approximately 25% of those with the disorder; however, most children who developed seizures had IQ scores less than 50, while few with higher intelligence did.

Fifth digit Coding
0 = full syndrome currently present
1 = full syndrome occurred previously; only residual symptoms pres-

ent, such as blunted or inappropriate affect, social withdrawal, or eccentric behavior.

Axis V. Highest level of adaptive functioning. Social awkwardness and ineptness persist even in residual state and adequate social adjustment is primarily dependent on IQ and development of language skills.

PERVASIVE DEVELOPMENTAL DISORDERS: DSM-III CODES AND DIAGNOSTIC CRITERIA

Pervasive Developmental Disorders: DSM-III Codes
Fifth digit code 0 = full syndrome present 1 = residual state 299.0(x) Infantile autism 299.9(x) Childhood onset pervasive developmental disorder 299.8(x) Atypical

Characteristic of Pervasive Developmental Disorders is distorted development of multiple basic psychological functions involving the development of language and social skills such as attention, perception, and motor movement. The core disturbance affects many of these areas at the same time and to an abnormal degree. Initial diagnostic differences exist between these disorders and Dementia or Schizophrenia. Dementia (corresponding to the ICD-9 category of Disintegrative Psychosis) includes behavioral abnormalities such as rapid loss of language and social skills, whereas PDD is characterized by an initial abnormality in the development of such skills. Schizophrenics might exhibit oddities of behavior similar to PDD, but there is also the presence of hallucinations, delusions, loosening of associations, or incoherence.

**Infantile Autism: Essential Features
and Differential Diagnosis**

---

i. Onset before 30 months of age
Determination of onset of symptoms is crucial in making this diagnosis. Childhood Onset PDD occurs after 30 months of age and does not typically show the full autistic syndrome. In making this type of diagnostic distinction retrospectively, however, the accuracy of reported age of onset is often difficult to establish without clinic records.

ii. Pervasive lack of responsiveness to other people
Initially, this deficit may be thought to be due to hearing impairment, and in the young infant an audiogram can easily determine if this is the case. The hearing-impaired child will consistently respond to loud sounds whereas the autistic child's responses are inconsistent. Lack of responsiveness is sometimes difficult to assess in the youngster who has developed superficial skills or shows attachment behavior through continuous association with a caretaker. It is up to the clinician to establish his/her own guidelines for evaluating social relatedness, especially in an older child.

iii. Gross impairment in communication skills
The autistic child retains such a pervasive lack of responsiveness that differential diagnosis of a child with Developmental Language Disorder, Receptive Type is easily made by observing attempts to communicate through gesture, to make eye contact, etc.

iv. Peculiar speech patterns if speech is present

v. Bizarre response to aspects of the environment
Differentiation between autism and other disorders which show behavioral oddities will depend on the extent to which other characteristic symptoms are present or absent, i.e., Childhood Onset PDD, Atypical PDD, Schizotypal Personality Disorder, Schizophrenia, or Mental Retardation.

(continued)

Infantile Autism: (continued)

---

vi. Absence of delusions, hallucinations, loosening of associations, and incoherence
In Schizophrenia, evidence of psychotic features *must* be present for diagnosis. Also, no increased incidence of Schizophrenia is found in the familial histories of autistic children.

Mental retardation is an additional diagnosis for some autistic children, as 40% are reported to have IQ scores less than 50. This is an issue that needs future clarification. In some cases it may be a matter of a test's inability to compute equivalent IQ scores for the nonverbal child; in others, the question is whether any distinction should be made if IQ is below 50. It may be helpful to note that the full autistic syndrome is rarely present in the child singularly diagnosed as mentally retarded.

Childhood Onset Pervasive Developmental Disorder: Essential Features and Differential Diagnosis

---

i. Gross and sustained disturbance of social relations
ii. Multiple oddities of behavior (must demonstrate three of those listed in the diagnostic criteria)
iii. Development of symptoms after 30 months and before 12 years of age
iv. Absence of psychotic features
None of the symptoms associated with impaired reality-testing, as in schizophrenia, are evident, although there may be presence of bizarre ideas and fantasies, preoccupation with morbid thoughts or interests, or pathological preoccupation with or attachment to objects

---

This type of disorder has a common association with low IQ and a concomitant diagnosis of Mental Retardation is indicated if clinical description matches diagnostic criteria for that disorder. In Schizotypal Personality Disorder, symptoms may exhibit similar oddities of behavior and speech, but the profound disturbance of social relations present in Childhood Onset PDD is absent, as well as disturbances of motor movement, inappropriate affect, and self-mutilation.

Fifth digit codes should be used to indicate presence of full syndrome (0) or residual symptoms (1).

Axis V. Highest level of adaptive functioning. There is frequent inability for children with this disorder to achieve any type of independent functioning.

Atypical Pervasive Developmental Disorder
This category is reserved for cases in which classification precludes Infantile Autism or Childhood Onset PDD. Refer to those sections for diagnostic features and differential diagnosis. Use the fifth digit code to indicate presence of full syndrome or residual symptoms.

MENTAL RETARDATION: A DIFFERENTIAL OR CONCURRENT DIAGNOSIS

Mental Retardation: DSM-III Codes
Fifth digit code 1 = With other behavioral symptoms (requiring attention or treatment and that are not part of another disorder) 0 = Without other behavioral symptoms 317.0(x) Mild mental retardation, IQ 50–70 318.0(x) Moderate mental retardation, IQ 35–49 318.1(x) Severe mental retardation, IQ 20–34 318.2(x) Profound mental retardation, IQ Below 20 319.0(x) Unspecified mental retardation

It is important to code other Axis I mental disorders. Ones commonly associated with Mental Retardation include: Stereotyped Movement Disorder, Infantile Autism, Attention Deficit Disorder with Hyperactivity, and Pervasive Developmental Disorder. The question remains, however, whether such coding is meaningful when IQ is below 50.

On Axis II, the clinician should code any Specific Developmental Disorders (in cases of mild retardation) if continued development shows specific deficits.

On Axis III, any physical disorders and conditions are recorded, including any known biological factor of etiological significance and any neurological abnormalities.

**Mental Retardation: Essential Features
and Differential Diagnosis**

---

i. Subaverage intellectual functioning as defined by IQ less than 70

Clinical judgment may permit flexibility in using the indicated cutoff points depending on the degree of impairment, adaptive functioning, and individual considerations. IQ scores have an error of measurement of approximately five points (i.e., 70 = 65 to 75). A V Code, Borderline Intellectual Functioning, is also indicated for IQ range of 71–84.

In Mental Retardation, the quality of impaired development seems to follow normal stages but lags far behind and may be arrested at early levels. However, this condition can coexist with Specific or Pervasive Developmental Disorders. Before coding multiple diagnoses, be sure to check the essential features for those classes. In cases where IQ is below 50, such multiple diagnoses would be meaningless.

ii. Impaired adaptive behavior

If IQ scores fall within the range of 71–84 and there are deficits in adaptive functioning due to intellectual impairment, consider the V Code for Borderline Intellectual Functioning.

iii. Onset before age 18

A differential diagnosis of Dementia is required if onset is after age 18, but if onset occurs before age 18 and previous intellectual functioning has been normal, both Dementia and Mental Retardation are coded.

When considering the presence of an additional disorder, the examiner must first account for all the symptomatology that can be primarily attributed to mental retardation.

REACTIVE ATTACHMENT DISORDER OF INFANCY

The Reactive Attachment Disorder of Infancy is considered in the same chapter as PDD primarily because we felt that, for differential diagnosis, comparing it with a group of disorders encountered during the first years of life and encompassing developmental abnormalities was more appropriate than keeping it as an isolated subject.

**Reactive Attachment Disorder of Infancy:
Essential Features and Differential Diagnosis**

i. Onset prior to eight months

ii. Lack of adequate care thus hindering the development of affectional bonding

iii. Lack of age-appropriate signs of social responsiveness (DSM-III lists deficits)

iv. Shows at least three of the behaviors listed in DSM-III as indicative of the syndrome

v. Failure to make age-expected weight gains

vi. Not accounted for by physical disorder, Mental Retardation or Autism

vii. Confirmation of diagnosis is reversal of symptom picture in response to treatment intervention

Differentiation should be made from children with severe neurological abnormalities or with severe and chronic physical illness, as they may demonstrate minor disturbances in social responsivity or developmental abnormality. In psychosocial dwarfism onset is often later than eight months and shows failure to gain in length rather than weight.

By definition, Reactive Attachment Disorder of Infancy is a condition evidenced by impaired emotional and physical development prior to the age of eight months and directly attributable to inadequate caretaking. Prominent deficits are failure to express age-appropriate signs of social responsivity and failure to gain the expected amount of weight for the given age. The condition usually responds positively to nurturing and adequate care. It is not the result of a physical disorder, Mental Retardation, or Infantile Autism. There may be cases in which Mental Retardation or Infantile Autism would be diagnosed in addition to Reactive Attachment Disorder of Infancy. The major distinction between Mental Retardation, Infantile Autism, and Reactive Attachment Disorder is that in the latter there is medical evidence for lack of care which is directly responsible for the condition.

While DSM-III recognition of a syndrome that has an honorable tradition in child psychiatry research is a welcomed gesture, there are aspects of the diagnosis that are bound to create problems. One difficulty, for instance, involves the continuing controversy which surrounds the age at which a diagnosis can and should be made. DSM-III states that this particular diagnosis can be made as early as in the first month of life. Another complication arises in the way DSM-III implicates interference in early emotional bonding as a predisposing factor in the condition, when it is difficult to establish with any objectivity that affectional bonds are actually formed in the infant. This in turn poses the question of whether or not we have any business basing a diagnosis on bonding interference when we specify that the interference must occur before an age in which specific attachments are clearly manifest (Rutter & Shaffer, 1980). In addition to these niggling arguments, there is a seemingly more serious flaw that Rutter and Shaffer have pointed out.

Response to treatment as confirmation of diagnosis can be assumed in part, but to conclude that treatment response defines a diagnosis and to include such a condition with the diagnostic criteria for Reactive Attachment Disorder seems premature and hopelessly begs the question, while creating a false validity. Proper examination of outcome through follow-up is needed to determine if complete reversal of the Reactive Attachment Disorder of Infancy is achieved by simply providing adequate care at time of initial diagnosis, as implied in DSM-III. It may be that treatment response is only partial. Description of the course of illness only concedes that, in absence of severe physical complications, emotional impairment will be limited to the effects that the child's environment may have on personality development. How is objective evidence collected which will determine whether or not there are repercussions or eventual long-term side effects in individuals with this diagnosis? If complete reversal is for the most part possible, does this not cast doubt on the assumption that basic attachment behavior causes the emotional dysfunction and lack of social responsivity comprising the illness? In any case, the focus must be on the elimination of continuing social stressors and noxious environmental factors. Thus, the use of Axis IV may become very important in the diagnosis and treatment of this particular disorder.

Rutter and Shaffer make a further point about DSM-III's specification that a similar clinical condition with onset *after* eight months of age should be diagnosed as Major Depression if symptoms are within the criteria specified for that disorder. Since there are often indications of depression within the maternal caretaker, it may be interesting to examine the genetic component in relation to depression in children with this same symptom pattern—regardless of age of onset, but within, say, the first two years of life—with follow-up for depression later in childhood, adolescence, and adulthood. Who knows whether or not a genetic component in combination with environmental factors, or something as simple as alcohol use in the mother, may upset the notion of affectional bonds altogether (or establish its place once and for all).

CASE VIGNETTE: HELEN

Helen, an eight-month old, was referred by her caseworker before placement in foster care. She was in the 15th percentile for weight, although length was normal. The caseworker was struck by Helen's sad expression and lack of interest in toys or visitors. Her existence had been chaotic since birth. Born to a chronic paranoid schizophrenic mother, who was now reinstitutionalized, her father unknown, Helen had had minimal care from her mother and only begrudging ministrations from a landlady who had taken tenuous claim of her with the exacerbation of the mother's illness. The mother had been hallucinating and delusional since Helen's birth and it was doubtful if she would ever be able to provide the adequate care the infant needed. During the examination, Helen was apathetic and disinterested in the examiner. She made no sounds. Motor development was normal.

Six months after placement in a foster home, Helen's weight had increased to the 50th percentile, she had begun to exhibit a few signs of responsiveness toward the foster mother, and she vocalized some sounds. She was fearful, however, and cried periodically without apparent cause.

Diagnosis

Axis I: 313.89 Reactive Attachment Disorder of Infancy
Axis II: None
Axis III: None
Axis IV: Extreme—6
Axis V: Not applicable

Discussion

Evidence of the disorder is confirmed by medical examination. There is history of neglect. Partial improvement of symptoms shows response to more favorable conditions. It seems unlikely, however, that Helen can achieve complete recovery from these disastrous circumstances, as she may already qualify for a second diagnosis of Major Depression. Environmental circumstances may play a major role in treatment planning.

This case illustrates the relative uselessness of Axis V for many child cases. Axis IV would be more useful if a particular stressor was given. Note that Axis V as used in the British system (see Appendix I) would be most useful, allowing a coding of 01.—mental disturbance in other family members. The DSM-III Axis V, highest level of functioning, is most applicable for disorders that are rarely diagnosed in childhood!

CASE VIGNETTE: LITTLE FLIPPER

Jason is an attractive 5½-year-old youngster who shows significant delays in social and self-help skills. He makes sounds but as yet has not formed words. At times he engages in peculiar finger movements and will flap his hands when he is either very happy or angry. His parents report that sometimes he is fleetingly cuddly; but he does not play appropriately or tolerate other children very well. Inappropriate behaviors make him a management problem and he often has temper tantrums and screams without cause. He does not react to spankings and if injured does not cry. His minor daily rituals are tolerated by his family, but interruptions cause him considerable distress. At this point he does not yet dress himself and wears diapers day and night. He is very attached to a stuffed teddy bear but easily separates from his mother. Often he will engross himself for long periods twirling a tissue or blades of grass in front of his face. His parents are concerned that his obliviousness to danger may cause him harm unless he is constantly supervised. They report that he rarely complies with expected tasks.

Jason was 18 months old when his parents began to suspect that he was different. He seemed too good and, at the same time, not responsive enough. A hearing evaluation was normal.

On a recent clinic visit Jason continued to display poor social relatedness and very superficial skills. He easily took the interviewer's hand and did not seem to discriminate between his mother and strangers. An occasional grimace momentarily altered his somewhat bland expression and he appeared tuned out and disinterested in most things about him. The background noise in the clinic agitated him and he frequently put his fingers in his ears. When he was upset, he butted his head against his mother and resisted tactile contact.

Diagnosis
  Axis I: 299.00 Infantile Autism, Full Syndrome
  Axis II: None
  Axis III: None
  Axis IV: None—1
  Axis V: Grossly impaired—7

Discussion
Jason exhibits the characteristic symptoms of Infantile Autism. Onset before 30 months and Jason's lack of responsiveness, odd behaviors and absent language make this diagnosis straightforward. It is important that the *observer* rate relatedness, however, as parents often offer their own interpretation of the child's relatedness, which may not agree with the child's relatedness as seen by others. Evaluation of intellectual functioning has ruled out Mental Retardation.

Chapter 10

Schizophrenia and Other Disorders With Psychotic Features

Schizophrenia is primarily a disorder of young adulthood and for this reason has not been included in the DSM-III section on Disorders Usually Evident in Infancy, Childhood, or Adolescence. However, its relatively frequent occurrence in late adolescence, as well as the considerable debate about the use of this diagnosis for children, prompts further discussion of the application of this definition in pediatric diagnosis.

DSM-III DEFINITION OF SCHIZOPHRENIA

Use of the Term "Psychotic"
DSM-III has, for the first time, clearly defined subtypes of schizophrenia and carefully distinguished them from other disorders. A primary concept is the term "psychotic," which describes a broad range of behaviors marked by gross impairment in reality-testing. The term can be applied to behavior or can indicate the phase of a disorder in which the behavior occurs. When this condition exists, the individual is unable to correctly evaluate the accuracy of his/her perceptions and thoughts and therefore makes incorrect assumptions about external reality. Evidence of this process in schizophrenia is characterized by delusions or hallucinations,

grossly disorganized behavior, or incoherent speech. The specific symptoms cited in DSM-III criteria for schizophrenia are characterized by disruption of numerous psychological functions (DSM-III, pp. 182–184, 188–189). At least one must be present during a phase of the illness in order to receive diagnosis for schizophrenia.

Psychotic characteristics are evident in disorders other than schizophrenia and imply impaired reality testing. DSM-III psychotic disorders include Pervasive Developmental Disorders, Paranoid Disorders, some Affective Disorders and Organic Mental Disorders, and Psychotic Disorders Not Elsewhere Classified. Within each of these categories there are specific guidelines concerning the nature of the psychotic features; these guidelines must be closely observed for differential diagnosis. This subtle distinction is important for diagnostic differentiation between psychotic disturbance and Mental Retardation or Pervasive Developmental Disorder within the pediatric age group. For this reason, the childhood category PDD was redefined in a way that more accurately describes the abnormal conditions.

The DSM-III clinical criteria for schizophrenia include a characteristic symptom picture encompassing deterioration in social and occupational functioning in which the clinical course follows a typical pattern with a minimum six-month duration.

If duration is less than two weeks and in response to a stressor, a diagnosis of Brief Reactive Psychosis is considered. Duration of more than two weeks but less than six months would be considered Schizophreniform Disorder. In the event that the latter two disorders, which are exactly the same as schizophrenia except for duration, should extend past the specified duration time, the diagnosis would change accordingly.

A diagnosis of Affective Disorder should take precedence if there is a prominent disturbance of mood prior to onset of psychotic features. When this differentiation is too difficult to determine, the category of Schizoaffective Disorder may be indicated.

With adolescents especially, it is important to rule out a substance-induced Organic Delusional Syndrome, especially during an initial, floridly psychotic episode. Duration will also be an important differentiator, although substance abuse may be a precipitating factor in the onset of a more serious condition.

If Mental Retardation is present, Schizophrenia can be diagnosed only if there are sufficient symptoms present that are not accounted for by retardation, in which case a multiple diagnosis is appropriate.

**Schizophrenia: Essential Features
and Differential Diagnosis**

---

i. Presence of at least one psychotic feature during the active phase of the illness

Schizophrenia always involves the presence of delusions, hallucinations, or disturbances in the form of thought disorder during some phase of the illness. Characteristic symptoms involve multiple psychological processes, including content of thought and thought processes, perception, affect, sense of self, volition, relationship to the external world, and psychomotor behavior.

ii. Deterioration from previous level of functioning
iii. Onset before age 45

Onset usually occurs during adolescence or early adulthood. There is some question as to the incidence of this disorder in younger children, although the PDD diagnosis applies to the majority of younger children who exhibit impairment in reality-testing.

iv. Duration of at least six months

This time period must include an active symptom phase with some sign of the illness still present, though it need not include prodromal or residual stages. The active phase is often associated with a psychosocial stressor.

If systematically organized persecutory or jealous delusions are present but there is no other evidence of hallucinations or more bizarre delusions or disordered thinking, a diagnosis of Paranoid Disorders is considered. Paranoid Disorders feature an organized delusional system in an otherwise more or less intact individual and are not usually diagnosed in younger children. In Paranoid Disorders, the marked drop in level of functioning which is necessary for the diagnosis of Schizophrenia does not usually occur.

Psychotic Disorders Not Elsewhere Classified include Brief Reactive Psychosis, Schizophreniform Disorder, Schizoaffective Disorder, and Atypical Psychosis. These are of little importance for consideration in childhood diagnosis, with the exception of Schizophreniform Disorder, which may occur with some frequency in adolescence. These and other differential diagnoses are discussed more extensively in DSM-III, which should be consulted if necessary. They include:

- Organic Mental Disorder
- Organic Delusional Syndrome
- Paranoid Disorders
- Affective Disorders
- Schizoaffective Disorder
- Obsessive Compulsive Disorder
- Hypochondriasis
- Phobic Disorders
- Personality Disorders

TYPES OF SCHIZOPHRENIA:
DSM-III CODES AND DIAGNOSTIC CRITERIA

Axis I. Schizophrenic Disorders: DSM-III Codes
295.1x Disorganized
295.2x Catatonic
295.3x Paranoid
295.9x Undifferentiated
295.6x Residual

The classification of the course of the illness is coded in the fifth digit, as follows:

(1) *Subchronic.* More or less continuous signs of the illness including prodromal, active, and residual phases are apparent for at least six months but less than two years.

(2) *Chronic.* Same course as above for more than two years.

(3) *Subchronic with Acute Exacerbation.* Residual phase is followed by

recurrence of prominent psychotic symptoms in subchronic course.
(4) *Chronic with Acute Exacerbation.* Residual phase is followed by recurrence of prominent psychotic symptoms in chronic course.
(5) *In Remission.* Used when individual no longer displays signs of
illness for a period of time.
(6) *Unspecified.*

Axis II. Record premorbid personality disorder if known. Follow
coding with (Premorbid).
Axis IV. Record any psychosocial stressor that may have been associated with onset.
Axis V. Record previous level of functioning. One often sees deterioration from previous level in areas of functioning such as performance of expected duties, social relations, and self-care.

Schizophrenia Subtypes: Essential Features and Differential Diagnosis

a. *Disorganized*
Incoherence and silly affect, accompanied by associated oddities of behavior and social impairment, are considered the most prominent features of this type of schizophrenia. Onset is typically early and insidious with a
chronic course.

b. *Catatonic*
The most striking thing about this subtype is psychomotor disturbance. Mutism is also common.

c. *Paranoid*
This subtype is marked by the prominence of delusions as indicated previously. A person with this disorder
is likely to be argumentative and at times violent; he/she
may show generalized anxiety. Doubts of gender identity
are commonly expressed. In Paranoid Disorders, the delusions are more systematized and believable and there is
absence of hallucinations, thought disorder, or disoriented
behaviors.

Schizophrenia Subtypes *(continued)*

---

d. *Undifferentiated*
Symptoms cannot be classified in any of the other subtypes or more than one of the subtypes describes the disorder.

e. *Residual*
The clinical picture may resemble residual Pervasive
Developmental Disorders in some cases, but this should
be easily cleared up by checking case history, since in Pervasive Developmental Disorders there is no occurrence of
delusions, hallucinations, incoherence, or marked loosening of associations. This code is used when the patient is
without prominent psychotic symptoms, but signs of the
illness persist.

USE OF THE DIAGNOSIS WITH CHILDREN
In DSM-II, Childhood Schizophrenia was the only category referring to
psychotic disorders of childhood. Now, DSM-III categories include the
Pervasive Developmental Disorders as well as Schizophrenia, which is not
particularly distinguished for children. DSM-III seeks to make a clear distinction between Schizophrenia and Infantile Autism, on the assumption
that the best available evidence indicates that they are two distinct disorders (Rutter & Schopler, 1978).

In childhood, Schizophrenia is less clearly differentiated by separate
subtypes. Kanner (1962) emphasized, for example, that there is less content and less variability clinically than with adult patients; he focused instead on emotional withdrawal, diminished interest in the environment,
alterations in motility patterns, and perseverations or stereotypy. There
is considerable debate about the manifestation of Schizophrenia specific
to childhood. Some writers (e.g., Cantor, Evans, Pearce, & Pezzot-Pearce,
1982) argue for validity of a separate category of childhood schizophrenia,
suggesting that these children have age-specific impairments of the motor
system, that the disorder can be manifest before 30 months of age, and that
abnormal thought processes and content become manifest between ages
of three and five, when appropriate language development should occur.

Differentiation Among Schizophrenia, Pervasive Developmental Disorders, and Infantile Autism

In practice, DSM-III has gone about dealing with this controversial problem in the most straightforward way. The best validated category, that of Infantile Autism, is clearly defined by early onset (before 30 months), pervasive lack of responsiveness, and gross deficits in language development. Furthermore, there must be a lack of delusions, hallucinations, loosening of asssociations, and incoherences, which clearly distinguish it from Schizophrenia. There remains some controversy around this distinction, however, as Fish (1977) argues for continuity between the conditions.

Childhood Onset Pervasive Developmental Disorder defines a category about which the least is known. For this category, the essential features (see section in Chapter 9 on Pervasive Developmental Disorder) emphasize gross impairment in social relationships and major impairment in the development of multiple basic psychological functions, but there must also be an absence of delusions, hallucinations, incoherence, or marked loosening of associations. The relationship between Childhood Onset Pervasive Developmental Disorder, as defined in DSM-III, and the disorder of childhood schizophrenia proposed by Cantor and others is at this time unclear. However, by providing clear definitions, DSM-III has provided the tools for empirically testing the validity of the category. A follow-up study of a group of children so defined has yet to be undertaken.

In practice, difficulties may frequently arise when clinicians are faced with the atypical case or with children between the ages of three and seven. A pragmatic task for clinicians is to decide whether or not a diagnosis of thought disorder can be made or how presence or absence of hallucinations and delusions should be assessed in the nonverbal child. If a nonverbal child appears to be watching something on the ceiling, for example, when the examiner can see nothing, should the diagnosis of visual hallucinations be made? Similarly, how can one assess cognitive incoherence in children with speech abnormalities? Unless thought disorder, hallucinations, or delusions can be shown without a doubt, it is suggested that Childhood Onset or Atypical Pervasive Developmental Disorder be diagnosed in young children (i.e., onset before age 12).

Differentiation From Other Categories

When differentiating the disorders discussed above from Schizoid Disorder of Childhood or Adolescence, the clinician should note that this latter classification is reserved for those children with social isolation of a consistent and chronic nature, who do not have formal thought disorder or show the deterioration seen in Schizophrenia or psychotic disorders. The diagnosis of Schizoid Disorder is more easily distinguished from Avoidant Disorder of Childhood or Adolescence because in the latter condition social relations within the family are considered normal and satisfying.

SCHIZOID DISORDER OF CHILDHOOD OR ADOLESCENCE (313.22)

Generally speaking, this disorder is the equivalent of Schizoid Personality Disorder used if the patient is 18 or older. (*Note:* Schizoid Personality Disorder can be diagnosed in individuals 18 and under. However, it is hard to judge if such a behavioral pattern is established before age 18 or older.)

Schizoid Disorder of Childhood or Adolescence: Essential Features and Differential Diagnosis

The principal feature of Schizoid Disorder of Childhood or Adolescence is consistent social isolation, without friendship or pleasure in social activities. Even within the family, relationships are isolated and, if existent, usually limited to dependence on one family member.

The most noticeable characteristic of this disorder is social isolation and little desire on the part of the child for social involvements, especially with peers. Instead, such children prefer to absorb themselves in their own thoughts or daydreams, but show no loss of reality-testing. Belligerent or aggressive behaviors, if any, tend to stem from demands requiring social interaction. These qualities will influence differential diagnosis. In Avoidant Disorder of Childhood, the lack of social contact arises from anxiety over participating in social activities. Since no psychotic features are evident, Pervasive Developmental Disorder and Schizophrenia are exclusionary criteria, though this disorder may predispose onset of Schizophrenia for some individuals. It also lacks the antisocial behavior associated with Conduct Disorder, Undersocialized, Nonaggressive.

(continued)

Schizoid Disorder of Childhood or Adolescence
(continued)

In making a differential diagnosis between this disorder and Schizophrenia, it should be noted that the latter involves an obvious disorder of thinking, with deterioration of social behavior. In Pervasive Developmental Disorders, there is impairment of language, often other bizarre behaviors such as atypical movements, and usually more gross impairment. In Avoidant Disorder of Childhood, relationships are normal and satisfying within the family.

It is interesting that Schizoid Disorder does not exclude some of the oddness that might appear, for example, in the adult diagnosis of Schizotypal Personality Disorder and so might be used to encompass a somewhat wider group of children who do not meet the criteria for psychotic disorder. As yet there are no useful data on this group.

CASE VIGNETTE: ROOTS

Stephen, age 15, was a good student, played chess and checkers and kept a garden in the family suburban home. Mother was very controlling toward all the children and required them to spend a lot of their free time visiting her elderly relatives. She and Stephen's father, a rather withdrawn man, disagreed openly about childrearing and most other subjects. Stephen's older sister had emancipated herself after a violent, probably irrevocable break with the family. Stephen had always wet the bed at least once a week, which was painfully embarrassing to him.

Since age 12, Stephen had avoided all companions. At age 14, however, he had received honorable mention in school because of a paper he had written tracing his ancestors back 10 generations, discussing the importance of knowing one's roots. He was not pleased at the attention and stopped going to school. Over the following 10 months, Stephen became progressively bizarre, keeping notebooks in the cellar and wondering if there were ancestors buried there. His parents had been proud of his scholarship but finally became alarmed when he began to dig in the cellar looking for traces of these early burials.

Over the following year, Stephen gradually became more silent, developing odd jerks of the head and chewing movements of the jaw. He was finally sent to a state hospital where he became mute, soiling and sometimes smearing feces.

Diagnosis

Axis I: 295.92 Schizophrenia, Undifferentiated
307.60 Functional Enuresis, Primary
Axis II: None
Axis III: None
Axis IV: Moderate—4
Axis V: Very poor—6

Discussion

It is of interest that Stephen probably would have initially met diagnostic criteria for Schizoid Disorder of Childhood or Adolescence. Here too, the use of the British Axis V (02—Discordant intrafamilial relationships; see Appendix I) would be useful. Note that primary enuresis (also Axis I) predated the present illness and is one of a group of developmental delays slightly more common in high-risk children.

CASE VIGNETTE: WEATHERMAN

Evan is a 16-year-old, exceptionally good student, particularly in math and science. His parents, however, have been concerned since he was six or seven about his extreme social isolation and lack of affection. During grade school, he constructed a shortwave radio and spent most of his free time perfecting the design and listening to foreign stations. He became very interested in following the weather reports of different countries.

His recent fascination is satellite photographs of weather conditions around the world. In addition, Evan spends much time phoning various weather services and subscribes to several meteorological publications. He enjoys discussing the topic, but has little awareness of whether or not his audience is also interested. One or two friends briefly shared this interest, but have since dropped off and become interested in school activities.

Evan is emotionless and polite. Occasionally he expresses irritation over his parents' attempts to "interfere" in his affairs, though basically he considers them to be on his side, particularly his mother. Although he has no interest in sports, he is well coordinated and has no peculiarities of movement. He hopes to work at a weather station when he grows up and is particularly interested in working in the Antarctic.

Diagnosis
   Axis I: 313.22 Schizoid Disorder of Childhood or Adolescence
   Axis II: None
   Axis III: None
   Axis IV: None
   Axis V: Fair—4

Discussion
Evan's development as an infant was normal and his cognitive and language functioning developed normally; therefore, he would not fit criteria for Pervasive Developmental Disorder. He has no frank disturbance of thought and has no delusions or hallucinations, therefore not meeting criteria for Schizophrenia. Because his relationships within the family are distant, and because of his peculiar and intense interests, he does not resemble children with Avoidant Disorder of Childhood. Evan is irritable at times when disturbed, but has none of the antisocial behaviors that would be characteristic of Conduct Disorder and is, in fact, singularly honest and reliable with the limitations of his social abilities.

Chapter 11

Affective Disorders

DSM-III DEFINITION OF AFFECTIVE DISORDERS
Diagnosis of an Affective Disorder presupposes a primary disturbance of mood manifested by excessively high or low mood states and is not attributed to any other physical or mental disorder. DSM-III has grouped these disorders under three basic categories. Of these, Major Affective Disorders include Bipolar Disorder and Major Depression and require evidence of a full affective syndrome. Other Specific Affective Disorders are characterized by evidence of partial syndrome with duration of at least two years for adults; Atypical Affective Disorders cover those disorders that cannot be classified in either of the other two categories, such as Atypical Bipolar Disorder and Atypical Depression.

Diagnostic Criteria
The DSM-III criteria for the Affective Disorders, Major Depressive Episode, and Manic Episode are summarized in the following tables.

Essential Features and Differential Diagnosis
of the Affective Disorders
The basic difference between Bipolar Disorder and Major Depression is the occurrence of a manic episode. Cyclothymic and Dysthymic Disorders have symptoms characteristic of the manic and depressive syndromes but do not exhibit the specified duration and severity (see Tables 6 and 7). Atypical Bipolar Disorder and Atypical Depression are residual categories provided for those instances when manic or depressive features do not meet the clinical guidelines established for the other affective disorders.

TABLE 5
Major Affective Disorders: DSM-III Codes

	Subclassification by Fifth Digit Codes:
Major Depression	Major depressive episode

296.2x Single Episode	0 = Unspecified
296.3x Recurrent	2 = Without melancholia
	3 = With melancholia
	4 = With psychotic features
	(7 indicates unofficial non-ICD-9-CM fifth digit code for mood-incongruent psychotic features)
	6 = In remission

	Subclassification by Fifth Digit Codes:
Bipolar Disorder	Manic or mixed episode

296.6x Mixed	0 = Unspecified
296.4x Manic	2 = Without psychotic features
296.5x Depressed	4 = With psychotic features
	(7 indicates unofficial non-ICD-9-CM fifth digit code for mood-incongruent psychotic features)
	6 = In remission

Atypical Affective Disorders

296.70 Atypical Bipolar Disorder
296.82 Atypical Depression

Other Specific Affective Disorders

301.13 Cyclothymic Disorder
300.40 Dysthymic Disorder
(Also termed Depressive Neurosis)

TABLE 6
Major Depressive Episode: Summarized DSM-III Diagnostic Criteria

A. Dysphoric mood characterized by depression, irritability, hopelessness, or sadness that is prominent and consistent. (In children under age six, evaluate facial expression to determine dysphoric mood.)
B. In children under age six, three of the first four of the following symptoms must be present for a duration of at least two weeks; otherwise, four of the following symptoms must be present for two weeks:
   1. Lack of appetite or significant loss of weight.
      (In children under age six, evaluate expected weight gains.)
   2. Sleep disturbance.

TABLE 6 *(continued)*

3. Agitated or retarded motor activity.
   (Children under age six are more likely to be underactive.)
4. Lack of interest or pleasure in activities, social withdrawal.
   (Children under age six are likely to be apathetic when encouraged to engage in an activity.)
5. Tiredness, lack of energy.
6. Lack of self-esteem, feelings of worthlessness or self-reproach.
7. Indecisiveness, loss of concentration.
8. Suicidal thoughts or attempts, morbid thoughts.

C. No evidence of mood-incongruent delusions or hallucinations nor instances of bizarre behavior.
D. Does not meet criteria for Schizophrenia, Schizophreniform Disorder or Paranoid Disorder. Is not attributable to an Organic Mental Disorder or to Uncomplicated Bereavement.
   (See DSM-III for fifth digit coding and criteria for subclassification.)

TABLE 7
Manic Episode: Summarized DSM-III Diagnostic Criteria

A. One or several instances in which a prominent and persistent elevation in mood is exhibited. The mood elevation may be characterized by expansiveness or irritability, and at times may alternate with depression.
B. Three of the following symptoms must be prominent and persistent for a duration of at least one week. If the mood disorder is expressed by irritability, use four of the following symptoms.
   1. Increased activity and sociability (in comparison to usual patterns) or motor restlessness.
   2. Increased talkativity, persistent speech.
   3. Racing thoughts, flight of ideas.
   4. Grandiose, expansive, overly confident, intrusive.
   5. Decrease in amount of sleep needed, tireless.
   6. Easily distracted by irrelevant details, flighty.
   7. Increasingly careless and reckless without regard for consequences.
C. No evidence of mood-incongruent delusions or hallucinations or instances of bizarre behavior.
D. Does not meet criteria for Schizophrenia, Schizophreniform Disorder or Paranoid Disorder. Is not attributable to an Organic Mental Disorder such as Substance Intoxication. Is more severe than a hypomanic episode.
   (See DSM-III for fifth digit coding and criteria for subclassification.)

TABLE 8
Major Affective Disorders: Summarized DSM-III Diagnostic Criteria

1. Major Depression
   No history of manic episode but persistent and prominent dysphoric mood
   a. 296.2 Single episode
      One major depressive episode
   b. 296.3 Recurrent
      More than one major depressive episode as determined by the pres-
      ence of at least four DSM-III symptoms (p. 214).
      In children under age six, three out of the first four symptoms listed are
      required for the diagnosis.
2. Bipolar Disorder
   a. 296.4 Manic—Current or recent manic episode
   b. 296.5 Depressed
      1. One or more manic episodes by history
      2. Current or recent major depressive episode as determined by DSM-
         III criteria (p. 214).
   c. 296.6 Mixed
      1. Current or recent episodes of both manic and depressive episodes in
         rapidly alternating pattern.
      2. Prominent depressive symptoms lasting at least 24 hours.

TABLE 9
Dysthymic Disorder: Summarized DSM-III Diagnostic Criteria

A. During past year (for children and adolescents) has had symptoms characteristic
   of the depressive syndrome but not of severity and duration required for major
   depressive episode.
B. Symptoms relatively persistent or separated by short periods of normal mood.
C. Depressive periods marked by low mood, loss of interest or pleasure in usual
   activities.
D. Presence of three or more of the DSM-III symptoms (p. 223).
E. Psychotic features absent.
F. Depressed mood is clearly distinguished from the individual's usual mood, if
   there is preexisting disorder.

TABLE 10
Cyclothymic Disorder: Summarized DSM-III Diagnostic Criteria

A. For two years has had several periods in which displayed some depressive and
   manic symptoms but does not meet criteria for major depressive or manic episode.
B. Periods of normal mood intermixed or alternating with depressive or hypo-
   manic periods.
C. During depressive periods and hypomanic periods shows at least three of the
   DSM-III symptoms as specified (p. 220).
D. Psychotic features absent.
E. Not attributable to other mental disorder.
   (Cyclothymic Disorder may precede Bipolar Disorder.)

DIAGNOSIS OF DEPRESSION AND
OTHER AFFECTIVE DISORDERS IN CHILDREN

Mood disturbance in children has been a subject of considerable debate. There are those who maintain that age-specific criteria are important and necessitate a more inferential diagnosis on the part of the clinician, while others feel that a straightforward application of the adult diagnostic criteria is sufficient and valid in childhood. It is crucial for the diagnosis, however, that the mood disturbance be primary and not secondary to some other disorder. In childhood, a number of other disorders, such as Attention Deficit Disorder, Conduct Disorder, and developmental disabilities, are known to frequently and regularly produce at least some demoralization. Similarly, when mood disturbance is mild and appears to stem from acute psychosocial stress, a diagnosis of Adjustment Disorder should be made. If the quality of the mood disturbance is mild but chronic, however, Dysthymic Disorder is appropriate. Of the Affective Disorders, depression has been the most frequently identified, but there is growing evidence that mania is underdiagnosed in adolescents.

Much attention has been directed toward the diagnosis of depression in children in the past decade. Child psychiatrists generally agree on two facts: 1) that Major Depressive Disorder is less common in children than in adults, particularly in prepubertal populations; but also 2) that Major Depression has generally been underdiagnosed in children until the last few years.

DSM-III has carefully spelled out the diagnostic criteria for this group of disorders, with few, relatively minor modifications for children. For example, other specific affective disorders are characterized by a partial affective syndrome with a duration of at least two years. However, for children the duration has been shortened to one year for Dysthymic Disorder. Controversy remains over whether or not duration should be shortened for the other disorders as well. Similarly, children under age six need only show three rather than four essential features for major depressive episode. The most important distinction allowed for children under age six in the diagnosis of major depressive episode is that depressive mood may be inferred from persistently sad facial expression, without overt complaints of dysphoric mood. With these exceptions, the DSM-III criteria have been maintained across age groups. The rationale for this is that concepts such as "masked" depression or depressive "equivalents" have not been validated and do not seem necessary for current research models.

Several diagnostic patterns specific to childhood should be stressed. The Major Depressive Disorders have strong associations with both Conduct Disorder and Separation Anxiety Disorder in childhood. In contrast, the adolescent group seems to follow more closely the pattern of associated disturbance seen for adulthood disturbances. Additionally, in prepubertal children there is equal incidence in males and females for all of the Affective Disorders, while in older groups females predominate.

Dysthymic Disorder is still probably underutilized as a diagnosis in children. Frequently children with Attention Deficit Disorder, Conduct Disorder, Mental Retardation, or severe Specific Developmental Disabilities will have associated low self-esteem, tearfulness, and decreased enjoyment of activities. It is probable that the diagnosis of Dysthymic Disorder should be made more frequently in association with these other disorders. Use of multiple diagnoses would avoid the less fruitful either/or debate and an inappropriate use of Major Depressive Disorder as the sole diagnosis.

Mania is extremely rare in prepubertal children. Recently, however, there have been excellent studies pointing to the fact that the diagnosis of Mania in adolescents is overlooked by child psychiatrists. This oversight is quite striking, since analyses of patient charts suggest that patients clearly met the typical criteria for manic episode as outlined in DSM-III (Carlson & Cantwell, 1982). Increased awareness and alertness on the part of the clinician diagnosing adolescents may circumvent more severe complications, particularly in view of the possible benefits from lithium treatment, which might not be considered if the diagnosis of mania is not made.

In conclusion, Affective Disorders have probably been underdiagnosed in children, and research in this area was neglected until very recently. From what is known, it appears that Mania is underdiagnosed in adolescents and Major Depression is underdiagnosed in prepubertal children. In the latter group, males and females have equal incidence, and associated disturbances of Conduct Disorder, Separation Anxiety, or other disorders may be common.

CASE VIGNETTE: SAD AND BLUE

For the past three months, nine-year-old Eric has expressed fearfulness about attending catechism classes after school. In spite of excellent functioning in the studies, he becomes fearful at the prospect of spending three hours in the class. He reports a mixture of worries about failure and complains of stomachaches and headaches. Primarily, he feels sad, and for the past few weeks he has been unable to enjoy his usual school activities. Going to sleep is troublesome too, because he is worried about doing poorly in school and he frequently awakens several times during the night. At the same time, his school performance has begun to decline from all As to mostly B grades, both because of missing school and difficulty in concentrating on his work. He has become very blue and on several occasions he has burst into tears for no apparent reason.

His mother has had three depressive episodes. During the past 20 years of marriage the parents have had continuing marital problems. Eric and his two brothers have often been the center of their disputes. Although shy, Eric is a likeable child and has always been a good student. In the past, he has attended summer camp, and, though he was somewhat homesick, he seemed to enjoy the activities. He has stayed overnight several times with friends who live nearby, but does appear to be somewhat tied to his mother.

During the interview, Eric suddenly began to sob that he felt terrible all the time and several times said that he would be better off dead, although he denied any specific suicidal plan. He feels guilty that he's such a worry to his parents.

Diagnosis
> **Axis I:** 296.2 Major Depression, Single Episode
> 309.21—Separation Anxiety Disorder
> **Axis II:** None
> **Axis III:** None
> **Axis IV:** Moderate—4
> **Axis V:** Good—3

Discussion
Eric presents with symptoms of depression and separation anxiety. He meets criteria for Major Depression, Single Episode, while anxiety symptoms do not have sufficient severity or chronicity for the diagnosis of Anxiety Disorder. Here, too, the British Axis V choices of 02—Discordant intrafamilial relationships or 01—mental disturbance in other family members would be more informative clinically.

CASE VIGNETTE: SLEEPING SAMUEL
An 11-year-old black child named Samuel was referred to the child psychiatry clinic for attempted suicide. He had apparently concocted a mixture of medicines prescribed to his mother—antibiotics, sleeping pills, and aspirins—and consumed it in an attempt to kill himself. He slept at home

for almost two days; when he was finally awakened by his mother, she brought him to the hospital.

Samuel is from a poor inner-city neighborhood and since second grade has been in trouble repeatedly for stealing and breaking into empty houses. In school he has had academic difficulties and is assigned to a reading disability classroom for part of each day.

The mother is known to abuse alcohol and may also have been a prostitute. She has had several depressive episodes but has never been treated. Samuel's father has not been in contact with her since Samuel was born.

During the interview Samuel appeared sad and cried at one point, his thin shoulders shaking. He reported having severe blue periods which had been continuous for the past month. During blue periods he has thought that he might be better off dead. Recently, he has started to wake up in the middle of the night. He also indicated that of late he had been avoiding his usual neighborhood "gang."

Diagnosis
    Axis I: 296.23 Major Depression
            312.21 Conduct Disorder (Socialized, Nonaggressive)
    Axis II: 315.00 Developmental Reading Disorder
    Axis III: None
    Axis IV: Severe—5
    Axis V: Poor—5

Discussion
This case reflects the puzzling fact that childhood Major Depression is most commonly found in males who are frequently conduct disordered. In addition, there is the association between Conduct Disorder and Reading Disorder, which has been demonstrated so effectively by British epidemiological studies (Rutter et al., 1970). Here, too, British Axis 5 coding would indicate the associated abnormal psychosocial situations and would be more informative.

Chapter 12

Attention Deficit Disorder, Conduct Disorder, and Oppositional Disorder

Once again, we see that DSM-III has pulled apart the strands of a behavior disorder and reorganized it in smaller sections according to the flavor of the symptomatic behavior. By increasing the number of subtypes, it is also asking us to evaluate the usefulness of these distinctions. Because of the frequent association between the external problems exhibited in Attention Deficit Disorder (ADD), Conduct Disorder, and/or Oppositional Disorder, this kind of careful distinction enables appraisal of the salient features through follow-up observations among and within the disorders. For example, it is still uncertain whether or not Attention Deficit Disorder with Hyperactivity but without Conduct Disorder or significant aggressive behavior at age "A" would in itself constitute a significant mental health risk (for later Conduct Disorder or hyperactivity) at follow-up age "B." ADD without hyperactivity has been the major manifestation of the syndrome in girls, but again it is unclear whether or not this classification is a clinically significant predictor of difference in prevalence rates between sexes. There is also some indication that Oppositional Disorder may be a precursor of more severe types of behavior problems, later diagnosed as Conduct Disorder. The following discussion reviews the DSM-III criteria for each of these disorders.

ATTENTION DEFICIT DISORDER

Attention Deficit Disorder: DSM-III Codes
314.01 With Hyperactivity
314.00 Without Hyperactivity
314.80 Residual Type

Within this category the emphasis has shifted from hyperactivity to attentional problems, thus the change from the former DSM-II diagnosis of Hyperkinetic Reaction. Because an attention deficit is believed to be the signal feature of this syndrome, clinicians need to be able to evaluate or ascertain the degree of inattention in several different situations. Poor impulse control is closely associated with the attention problem, and excessive motor activity as an accompanying symptom is given an optional status within the three subtypes of this disorder. DSM-III has chosen to stress the prominence of attentional difficulties because they prevail for a longer period of time. Hyperactivity per se tends to diminish in adolescence. The course of the disorder typically follows one of three patterns: 1) all symptoms continue into adulthood with possible development of Antisocial Personality Disorder; 2) symptoms dissipate or disappear in adolescence; or 3) hyperactivity disappears but inattention and impulsivity persist into adolescence and adulthood. There have not been enough coded follow-up studies to record frequency patterns.

A child displaying these types of difficulties usually comes to the attention of professionals during the early school years, but parents often report onset by age three. In school, difficulties completing work and following or listening to directions increase because the situation demands sustained attention in a group setting where distracting stimuli are always present. Symptoms vary with time and place, home vs. school. Tasks requiring "self-application" are more likely to exacerbate symptoms than one-to-one relationships or new situations. The variability of the symptoms may require using multiple informants to obtain an overview of the problem. Primary consideration is given to the reports of teachers, however, because their views may be considerably more objective than those of the parents.

The number of symptoms required by the DSM-III criteria is specifically stated to be aimed at the eight-to-ten-year-old age group. If the child is younger, more symptoms would be expected; if older, less would be apparent.

Attention Deficit Disorder:
Essential Features and Differential Diagnosis

---

i. Inattention

Displays age-inappropriate symptoms regarding concentration, distractibility, task completion, and ability to listen. This occurs even when the child may be motivated to do the task.

ii. Impulsivity

Behavior patterns are characterized by impulsive conduct, including acting without thinking, quick changes of activity, inability to organize work, need of supervision, difficulty awaiting turn, and calling out in class.

iii. Hyperactivity

Quality of motor activity is excessive, non-goal-directed, and apparently beyond the child's control. The nature of the overactivity is different from that of a normal energetic child who would be able to direct behavior in a productive manner. Behavior may vary from fidgety, restless movement to inability to stay seated, or running and climbing as if "driven by a motor." Excessive movement may also be noted during sleep in some instances.

iv. Onset prior to age seven.

v. Duration exceeds six months.

vi. Not attributable to any other mental disorder, such as Schizophrenia, Affective Disorder, or Severe or Profound Mental Retardation.

Coding

Although DSM-III does not suggest a more limiting IQ cutoff, association with mild to moderate intellectual impairment is definitely possible and in such cases Mild to Moderate Mental Retardation should be coded. For research purposes, many centers are defining their own IQ limits in order to eliminate cases where factors contributing to the symptom pattern may be contaminated or largely determined by low intelligence.

Axis II. If ADD is coded as an Axis I disorder, one is often likely to encounter Axis II disorders within the category of Specific Developmental Disorders. These should be carefully coded because of the long association between ADD-type impairments and other developmental deficiencies.

Axis III. Diagnosable neurological disorders should be included on Axis III, along with other physical illness. In some research settings, a case with a known neurological impairment may be excluded as a means of protecting a "pure" classification of the syndrome under research. This occurs in only about 5% of the cases. "Soft" signs, however, are much more commonly noted, as well as motor/perceptual dysfunctions and EEG abnormalities.

Axis IV. Psychosocial stressors. These should always be coded, especially because the appearance of the same disorder within family groupings is more common than in the general population, and association with adult substance abuse and antisocial behaviors is seen among family members. Studies focusing on heritable and social factors are needed to help delineate the etiology of the syndrome more clearly.

Axis V. Adaptive functioning. This is important as well, as the ADD child frequently encounters academic difficulties which have implications for his or her future, as well as possibly exerting an effect on the course of the illness. It is also common for these children to experience problems in social functioning. Consideration given to this aspect of diagnosis will influence treatment interventions for social and academic problems, and outcome at follow-up may be predicted best by this measure.

Subtypes

The subtype ADD Without Hyperactivity is coded in the absence of hyperactivity as a salient feature, but must meet the DSM-III criteria for inattention and impulsivity. If there has been a well documented history of ADD with or without hyperactivity, ADD Residual Type is coded, even in adulthood. In such cases there must be some evidence of both attention deficit and impulsivity, resulting in a degree of impaired social or occupational functioning. Once again, the impairment is not due to Schizophrenia, Affective Disorder, Severe or Profound Mental Retardation, or Schizotypal or Borderline Personality Disorders.

Diagnostic Issues and Differential Diagnosis
The most difficult aspect of the ADD diagnosis is assessment of the extent of the inappropriate behaviors. DSM-III advises that the school report should be relied on more heavily in cases of discrepancy between parent and teacher opinion. Information is also supplied by the child through self-report or interview, direct observation of the child, indirect observation of the child through parent and teacher, and possibly psychological report or testing. These sources may not agree; thus, while DSM-III is specific in its guidelines, numerous decisions are required in order to make this frequent diagnosis. However, DSM-III does take a step toward helping us clarify what is meant by the hyperactive child.

Certain conditions may also constitute similar behaviors that should be distinguished from ADD. First consideration is age-appropriate overactivity, which is distinguished by the quality of the activity. By nature it would not be haphazard or disorganized. Another situation that may cause a child to simulate such behavior would be an inadequate, disorganized, chaotic environment. In all instances, the clinician must try to objectively evaluate all the circumstances surrounding the child. Specific learning disabilities may produce classroom restlessness, as can mild to moderate Mental Retardation or classroom placement mismatched to ability level. Other possibilities to eliminate are acute situational reactions or Adjustment Disorder. In these cases Axis IV and V should be helpful. Infantile Autism, Depression, and Schizophrenia preclude the use of this diagnosis. In the case of Mental Retardation (MR), only mild or moderate diagnoses should be double coded, and Profound or Severe MR would preempt an ADD diagnosis. Conduct Disorder (CD) and Oppositional Disorder (OD) may also be separately coded along with ADD on Axis I. (But one would not use both CD and OD together.)

CONDUCT DISORDER

Conduct Disorder: DSM-III Codes
312.00 Undersocialized, Aggressive
312.10 Undersocialized, Nonaggressive
312.23 Socialized, Aggressive
312.21 Socialized, Nonaggressive
312.90 Atypical

Diagnostic Criteria

The Conduct Disorder category has raised a lot of controversy concerning the validity of its subtypes, especially for application to prepubertal cases. Perhaps, as has been suggested, a more descriptive approach would involve indicating all the types of antisocial conduct exhibited, along with their frequency and severity. Nevertheless, the category is subdivided into four combinations of aggressive/nonaggressive, socialized/undersocialized types of behavior, based on some studies suggesting that independent syndromes and outcomes are determined by these distinctions. The nature of these behaviors is persistent and repetitive, their consequences being more serious than a mischievous prank. Milder forms tend to dissipate with maturity, but more severe forms are apt to be chronic.

Conduct Disorder:
Essential Features and Differential Diagnosis

The aggressive component requires a consistent pattern of aggressive activity violating the basic rights of others over a six-month period: violence against persons or property, or theft while confronting the victim. The nonaggressive component establishes a consistent pattern over a six-month period of nonaggressive activity violating the rights of others or social rules. Included are chronic disobedience of parental or school rules, running away from home, and persistent lying or stealing.

If social bonding is evident, the subtype is considered socialized. Attachments to others are judged to exist if the patient exhibits at least two of the following behaviors: peer-group friendships within a six-month period, extends self for others, feels appropriate guilt, is loyal to companions, and shows concern for their welfare. If only one of the aforementioned characteristics is observed, the subtype is considered undersocialized.

For patients over age 18, the diagnosis of Antisocial Personality Disorder must first be ruled out.

The subcategory Atypical is applied in those instances that elude classification under the specified types, but still display violation of societal norms and rights of others.

Other Axis I disorders often associated with Conduct Disorder are Attention Deficit Disorder and Substance Use Disorder. Axis II Specific Developmental Disorders are commonly found in conjunction with this category of illness. Social stressors on Axis IV often center on difficulties in the home or a family history of alcohol dependence and Antisocial Personality Disorder. Often economic factors, size of the family, and inconsistent or poor parenting are predisposing factors. On Axis V coding should evaluate academic and social functioning, as these are often areas of impairment.

Duration greater than a few months eliminates the question of diagnosing an Adjustment Disorder. Isolated instances of antisocial conduct, V Code 71.02 Childhood or Adolescent Antisocial Behavior, are relatively easy to distinguish from Conduct Disorders because they are usually limited in occurrence and do not show the lack of academic achievement and poor social relations that characterize the conduct-disordered child. (It is uncertain if onset of Explosive Personality Disorder begins in childhood, but this diagnosis should also be considered for the post-pubertal child.)

With Oppositional Disorder, similar characteristics of attitude may prevail, but without evidence of violation of the basic rights of others or major rules and social norms. Virtually all cases diagnosed as Conduct Disorder will meet the criteria for Oppositional Disorder; however, only the former diagnosis would be made.

If ADD or Specific Developmental Disorders are also present, they should also be coded on the appropriate axis. An Axis I diagnosis of Depression would also be coded.

Evidence of psychosis would preempt this diagnosis.

OPPOSITIONAL DISORDER

Oppositional Disorder: Essential Features and Differential Diagnosis
Oppositional Disorder, 313.81, entails persistent opposition to authority figures for a period of six months or more, characterized by a behavioral pattern of disobedient, negativistic, and provocative behaviors, particularly toward parents and teachers. Continually confrontive be-

(continued)

Oppositional Disorder: *(continued)*

---

havior is exhibited, even when it is destructive to the best interests or well-being of the patient. Such an individual rarely views the problem as originating within himself and his passive resistance to external authority often causes more discomfort for those around him than for him. The disorder interferes with social relationships and often results in academic failure and other school problems. Typically arising in late childhood or early adolescence, onset usually coincides with increased difficulties in relations with the family and use of illegal substances. The course is described as chronic, lasting for several years; it often continues in adulthood as a Passive-Aggressive Personality Disorder.

This diagnosis should not be used for children age 18–36 months when similar behaviors are considered normal. Conduct Disorder, as mentioned before, is characterized by violation of others' rights and societal norms, although Oppositional Disorder in some instances may be a precursor of CD. Schizophrenia and Pervasive Developmental Disorders preempt the use of this category. Instances of chronic Organic Mental Disorder and the mild to moderate forms of Mental Retardation may receive a double Axis I diagnosis. Attention Deficit Disorder has similar associated symptoms of obstinancy, stubbornness, negativism, temper outbursts, lack of response to discipline, etc. However , if the quality of these characteristics is more striking than in similar ADD cases, a double diagnosis of ADD and Oppositional Disorder should be given. If the subject is over the age of 18 and does not meet criteria for Passive-Aggressive Personality Disorder, this particular category should be documented.

A controversial issue concerning this diagnosis is one of degree, as it seems difficult to differentiate when the occurrence of these symptoms is normal, especially when viewing typical adolescent emancipation behaviors or temper outbursts in young children. Conscientious coding of this category, along with other applicable Axis I and II disorders, will help to determine the usefulness or validity of this category as a disorder.

A SUMMARY OF DIAGNOSTIC ISSUES
FOR THESE THREE CATEGORIES

There are several major concerns in considering DSM-III and Attention Deficit Disorder and Conduct Disorder. These assume great importance when one recognizes that these disorders together constitute well over 50% of the diagnoses at many, if not most, U.S. child guidance clinics. The debates focus around distinction from normality, the importance of discriminating between ADD and Conduct Disorder, and the splitting of subdiagnoses between and within ADD and CD.

Statements about abnormality vs. normality are usually based on judgments of symptom severity. DSM-III makes this easier for Conduct Disorder by defining relatively specific acts and for the most part clear social norms. For ADD, judgments about "often" or "easily" will be harder to make, particularly outside the classroom setting. The distinction between Conduct Disorder and ADD has not been stressed in European psychiatry. While ICD-9 has a category for Hyperkinetic Reaction, the diagnosis of Conduct Disorder requires "behavior giving rise to social disapproval," without relatively stringent rules as in DSM-III. Furthermore, the lack of acceptance of stimulant drug treatment in most of Europe has led to relative disinterest in identifying those restless and inattentive behaviors thought to best respond to stimulant medication.

Within the U.S., Conduct Disorder is clearly a valid and important diagnosis with significant follow-up risk (Robins, 1966). The significance of hyperactive behaviors without aggressiveness (i.e., inattentiveness, restlessness, impulsivity) for future prognosis is less clear, as most studies have had mixed groups and have, so far, found that aggressiveness, rather than the salient features of ADD, is the most powerful predictor of follow-up risk (Loney, Kramer, & Milich, 1981).

The tendency for ADD and OD to be used more often with younger children than CD may reflect a bias of the diagnostic criteria. It may now be "too hard" for younger children to fill criteria for CD. It is much more difficult to obtain a diagnosis of Conduct Disorder, aggressive type, because confrontation with a victim is involved. Furthermore, the major differentiation between socialized and undersocialized types of CD is based on friendship patterns of the child.

Means of assessing these characteristics are not indicated in the DSM-III guidelines and reliance on the clinician's good sense is not always the best way to objectively define a category of disorder. This relatively extreme definition of Conduct Disorder will certainly sift out the most severe cases. The usefulness of the category as a measure of disorder is still in question.

CASE VIGNETTE: REGINA

Six-year-old Regina has been brought to the clinic by her parents, who state that the child is ruining their marriage. The father feels that the mother spoils the girl with inconsistent discipline and the mother feels that she tries her best without success.

For at least the past three years, Regina has been "extremely difficult." She is willful and the "terrible twos" were never outgrown. Regina often spoils family treats planned for her by misbehaving and having friends sent home. At the private co-op school which she attends, the teachers often have her play quietly by herself because she irritates the other children. She lisps and talks baby talk, but this has improved slightly in the past year. Developmental milestones have been normal. She is considered quite bright in school. At the clinic interview, Regina enjoyed the individual attention shown her but was rather demanding in structuring the examination and tried to keep the playroom toys even though she was told that she couldn't.

Both parents are invested in the child but find her violent temper tantrums hard to handle.

Diagnosis
    Axis I: 313.81 Oppositional Disorder
    Axis II: 315.39 Developmental Articulation Disorder
    Axis III: None
    Axis IV: None Known—0
    Axis V: Fair—4

Discussion
Regina is best considered to have Oppositional Disorder, as she does not meet criteria for ADD or Conduct Disorder, possibly because of her relatively young age. It will be of considerable interest to see the eventual outcome for this girl, as the behaviors resemble some of those with passive-aggressive personality disorder. The parents are eager for counseling and it is hoped behavior therapy wil be helpful in shaping some positive behaviors. It is of interest that Regina has a mild articulation disorder which is associated with behavioral disturbance.

CASE VIGNETTE: REGINALD

Reginald, an 11-year-old black child was brought to the clinic by his mother (at the request of his school) because of continued fighting and bullying. His mother claims that Reginald has always been a "handful," but now feels that he gets out of line too often and that she can no longer control him. She recently found numerous items in his room which she believes to be stolen, and she has received several reports from neighbors about minor property damage. He lies constantly, even if caught and confronted. She attributes part of the problem to the influence of two older neighborhood boys with whom Reginald spends a lot of time. He was recently suspended from school along with these two friends for having set up a blockade to catch younger kids on the way home from school. The youths made small demands for money, but Reginald claimed that they intended no harm. There was, however, an incident in which a younger girl fell (or was pushed) off her bike.

Reginald has repeated both first and second grade. His teachers report that he is easily frustrated, is failing most subjects, and is constantly out of his seat creating a disruption. This kind of behavior is viewed as attention seeking. He works much better in the small resource class to which he is assigned two hours a day for help in reading. Most of the rest of his day is spent in the principal's office.

Reginald is the second oldest of four children in a one-parent home. His natural father left the home over a year ago, and the mother works two part-time jobs to make ends meet. This means that the children are left unsupervised a good part of the day, with Reginald's 15-year-old sister taking most of the responsibility. Reginald does not get along with this sister; he will hit and bite her if she tries to manage him.

The clinic evaluation testing showed that Verbal IQ = 57, Performance IQ = 78, and Full Scale IQ = 66.

Diagnosis
    Axis I: 312.23 Conduct Disorder, Socialized, Aggressive
              317.0 Mild Mental Retardation
    Axis II: 799.90 Diagnosis differed on Axis II
    Axis IV: Moderate—4
    Axis V: Poor—5, or very poor—6

Discussion
Reginald meets DSM-III criteria for Socialized Aggressive Conduct Dis-

order since the problems highlighted include a continued pattern of anti-social behavior: stealing (presumably from others), vandalism, and extortion.

His IQ testing indicates that his school placement is probably inadequate. In this case, Axis III coding, as in ICD-9, would insure that intellectual functioning was assessed.

Reginald also qualifies as mildly mentally retarded. It is possible that Reginald also has specific developmental difficulties, but the present data do not allow us to make this assessment. It is not clear if his level of academic backwardness is beyond that predicted by the behavioral disturbance together with the mild mental retardation. A V code would not be appropriate here (i.e., Academic Problem), because V codes are not intended for use on Axis II and are not used if there is an Axis I diagnosis.

CASE VIGNETTE: STUART

Eight-year-old Stuart was referred to the local child guidance clinic by his physician because of a history of overactivity, school problems, onset of illness within the family, and poor social relations.

The mother reported that Stuart was overly active as an infant and toddler. His teachers found him difficult to control once he started school. He is described as extremely impulsive and distractible, moving about tirelessly from one activity to the next. At present he knows his alphabet and a few words on sight, but he cannot read a full sentence. His math skills are also minimal. Because of these learning difficulties, Stuart is in a small, self-contained class for learning-disabled children. His teacher reports that he is immature and restless, responds best in a structured, one-on-one situation, but is considered the class pest because he is continually annoying the other children and is disobedient.

Since the start of the school year, he has soiled his pants on numerous occasions, does not seem to have any special friends, and has been reported on different occasions by the school bus driver for hitting other children and throwing things on the bus.

His mother reports that Stuart responds to some disciplining, but lately he has started sassing back and swearing at her. He frequently throws temper tantrums, especially if she asks him to do something or denies his requests. His constant badgering and whining are irritating for her, especially since her husband has been in and out of the hospital for the past six months with a terminal illness. Because of his illness, the father has been minimally involved with Stuart's discipline for the last two years.

Diagnosis

> **Axis I:** 314.01 Attention Deficit Disorder with Hyperactivity
> 318.81 Oppositional Disorder
> 307.70 Functional Encopresis
> **Axis II:** 315.00 Developmental Reading Disorder
> 315.10 Developmental Arithmetic Disorder
> **Axis IV:** Severe—5
> **Axis V:** Poor—5

Discussion

Stuart has symptoms typical of ADD with hyperactivity, as well as the additional burden of learning problems. His oppositional behavior (disobedience, throwing, hitting, tantrums) and soiling seem to coincide with the worsening of his father's illness. Because these behaviors have persisted for so long, diagnosis of Oppositional Disorder and Encopresis is made, and a stressor is recorded on Axis IV rather than using the diagnosis of Adjustment Disorder.

Chapter 13

Anxiety Disorders

The experience of anxiety and its resultant effects make up the major component of this group. Within the specific section of Anxiety Disorders of Childhood or Adolescence, the dysfunctions included are considered to be specific to that particular age group. These are Separation Anxiety Disorder, Avoidant Disorder of Childhood or Adolescence, and Overanxious Disorder. This discussion, however, also extends to Phobic Disorders and Obsessive Compulsive Disorder, which are featured in the Anxiety Disorders section of the DSM-III text and occur regularly (though not frequently) in children.

The acute anxiety state is experienced as an overwhelming sense of fear and dread that generally incapacitates the individual for a period of time. It may also induce physiological responses. Often it is initiated in response to certain stimuli or circumstances. Generalized anxiety is a more pervasive attitude of apprehension that keeps the individual in a constant state of vigilance. It is accompanied by signs of tension and autonomic arousal.

ANXIETY DISORDERS OF CHILDHOOD OR ADOLESCENCE

Anxiety Disorders of Childhood or Adolescence: DSM-III Codes
309.21 Separation Anxiety
313.21 Avoidant Disorder of Childhood or Adolescence
313.00 Overanxious Disorder

Fear of separation, social avoidance, and persistent worry are the major elements of the anxiety manifest within these disorders. Diagnosis of these disorders should be made when the manifest anxiety is the most salient feature, rather than being attributable to any other major disorder. In some cases there may be double coding as discussed below; however, these categories would never be used in conjunction with Pervasive Developmental Disorder, Schizophrenia, or other psychotic disorders.

Separation Anxiety
In Separation Anxiety, as the name suggests, anxiety is aroused upon separation from familiar persons, usually the parents, or upon leaving the home and entering new territory. The reaction is excessive and anticipated separation may induce somatic complaints or symptoms. After separation has occurred, the child may be inconsolable and express fears that the parent may not return or that some tragedy will ensue that will prevent the child from ever seeing the parent again.

Onset of this type of symptom pattern is often reported during the preschool years, but distinction must be made from a normal degree of separation anxiety that ensues during this age. The most extreme form of the disorder is reported to occur in prepubertal children, who may refuse to go to school in order to avoid the trauma of separation. DSM-III notes that this type of school refusal is only one instance in a variety of situations that the child tries to control in order to avoid separation from home or family. True school phobia entails a fear of the actual school setting and persists even if accompanied by the parent. Most instances of Separation Anxiety seem to develop in reaction to a major life stress (which should be noted on Axis IV) and follow a variable course of intensity for several years. An unexplained but common denominator in many of these cases is a close-knit, caring family constellation.

DSM-III spells out nine different descriptions of ways anxiety may be evidenced in this disorder and specifies that three of these symptoms must be present for a duration of two weeks. If the person is past age 18, this diagnosis is given only when the conditions for Agoraphobia are *not* met. While Separation Anxiety constitutes a type of phobic reaction, DSM-III characterizes it as a specific disorder of childhood and thus places it under the childhood disorders.

Avoidant Disorder of Childhood or Adolescence
This disorder is typified by a fear of strangers that predominates to such a degree that social functioning is impaired in an individual who otherwise displays appropriate and affectionate relationships with family mem-

bers and friends. Age-appropriate social interaction with peers is avoided; however, the degree of individual functional impairment is mild and may result only in feelings of loneliness or mild depression. The required duration is at least six months and age at onset must be greater than two and a half, since stranger anxiety is considered developmentally normal prior to that age. After age 18, this diagnosis is used only in the event that the individual fails to meet the criteria for Avoidant Personality Disorder. The course of the illness may show spontaneous improvement, appear in episodic sequences, or develop into a chronic pattern, though little information has been documented.

Differential diagnosis should take into account the shy, timid child who shows social reticence upon initial encounter but eventually warms up and is able to engage in age-appropriate peer interactions. A child with Separation Anxiety fears the separation more than the situation, and in Overanxious Disorder the anxiety is not limited to contact with strangers. The diagnosis is changed to Avoidant Personality Disorder if this pattern of impaired social relations has persisted for a long period of time and the individual is more than 18 years old. Adjustment Disorder with Withdrawal involves a recent social stressor and does not exhibit a historical pattern of impaired relationships. The discomfort displayed in Avoidant Disorder of Childhood does not exclude the desire for friendship and affection, whereas in Schizoid Disorder of Childhood or Adolescence a preference for social isolation is clearly indicated.

Overanxious Disorder
A child with this complaint exhibits anticipatory anxiety which is generalized to include most events requiring some form of judgment or appraisal of the child's performance or appearance. The child's behavior is likely to be characterized by restlessness, nervous habits, perfectionistic tendencies, and need for reinforcement and approval. Onset may be sudden or gradual and will tend to be exacerbated during periods of stress. If the condition persists into adulthood it may meet the conditions for Generalized Anxiety Disorder or Social Phobia. Occurrence is common in higher socioeconomic levels where performance expectations are high.

DSM-III itemizes a list of persistent worries and specifies that four be present for a period of six months in order to qualify for the diagnosis. The disturbance should not be diagnosed in association with Separation Anxiety Disorder, Avoidant Disorder of Childhood or Adolescence, Phobic Disorder, Obsessive Compulsive Disorder, Depressive Disorder, Schizophrenia, or a Pervasive Developmental Disorder. If Attention Deficit

Disorder is also evident, both diagnoses should be noted. Generalized Anxiety Disorder can only be applied if the individual is over 18 and has consistently exhibited the required behaviors for a period of time. If the criteria for the latter diagnosis are not met, and the individual is over 18, Overanxious Disorder may still be considered.

ANXIETY DISORDERS
The Anxiety Disorders, which are not specifically related to children, include the Phobic Disorders and Anxiety States. The subtypes applicable to the childhood and adolescent years are:

Anxiety Disorders: DSM-III Codes
300.23 Social Phobia
300.29 Simple Phobia
300.01 Panic Disorder
300.30 Obsessive Compulsive Disorder
308.30 Post-traumatic Stress Disorder, Acute
309.81 Post-traumatic Stress Disorder, Chronic or Delayed
300.00 Atypical Anxiety Disorder

Agoraphobia, with Panic Attacks (300.21) or without Panic Attacks (300.22), is presumed to be linked with childhood Separation Anxiety Disorder, and onset is usually not until late adolescence or early adulthood. Generalized Anxiety Disorder is only applicable as a diagnosis after age 18. The following discussion will highlight important features of these Anxiety Disorders as applied to the pediatric population.

Phobic Disorders
These subtypes involve a specific stimulus which, when encountered, initiates the anxiety response. Symptoms also include avoidance of the stimulus situations, objects, or activities which set off the anxiety response. Even though the subject may recognize the disproportionate emotion associated with the stimulus, continued and irrational avoidance of the anxiety source interferes with social and occupational functioning. When more than one type is present, multiple diagnoses are given.

Social Phobia. The common element of this phobia is a desire to protect oneself from situations in which others have the opportunity to observe. Such exposure to the view of others creates a continual fear of and wish to avoid such occasions because of possible humiliation and embarrassment. The individual usually fears only one type of situation and recognizes the irrationality of the fear and consequent reaction. Anticipatory anxiety only serves to strengthen phobic avoidance. In most instances the course is chronic, but rarely incapacitating. The disorder is not associated with Major Depression or Avoidant Personality Disorder, nor is it diagnosed in cases of Schizophrenia, Obsessive Compulsive Disorder, Simple Phobia, or Paranoid Personality Disorder.

Simple Phobia. The phobic reaction in this disorder is not attributable to potentially embarrassing or humiliating social situations, as in Social Phobia, or a fear of being alone or away from home, as is the case in Agoraphobia. The most common phobic stimuli encountered in individuals with this disorder are animals and fear of height or closed spaces. In all instances the disturbance is recognized as unreasonable distress and is not attributable to any other mental disorder. The diagnosis would not be used in cases of Schizophrenia or Obsessive Compulsive Disorder.

Anxiety States
Panic Disorder. The diagnosis requires at least three unpredictably recurring attacks of extreme anxiety within a three-week period. Although certain situations may be associated with the attack, the episode is not viewed as a response to a recognizable stimulus. Onset is precipitated by intense feelings of terror, apprehension, and impending doom. Anxiety symptoms experienced during the panic attack are outlined in DSM-III; four of them must be apparent for the diagnosis. The attack usually lasts several minutes, more rarely a couple of hours, but nervousness and apprehension, accompanied by physiological symptoms, may persist following the attack. The course is variable, both in length and severity. Sudden object loss is thought to be a predisposing factor and a history of Separation Anxiety Disorder may indicate susceptibility.

Differential considerations include the context of the complaint, as similar symptoms may arise after the extreme physical exertion of a life-threatening event, in which case a diagnosis is not designated. Some physical disorders (e.g., hyperthyroidism), as well as withdrawal or intoxication from certain substances, may also simulate symptoms. The diagnosis is also not given when panic attacks occur in conjunction with major mental disorders (Schizophrenia, Major Depression, Somatization Disorder). Generalized Anxiety Disorder is dismissed if there is evidence of panic attacks by history, although there may be some similarity initially because of the pervasive anxious quality that is evident in the interlude between episodes. In Panic Disorder, the anxiety attack may be provoked without encountering a known stimulus, and it is this quality which distinguishes it from Agoraphobia, and Simple or Social Phobia.

Obsessive Compulsive Disorder. Diagnosis of this disorder specifies the persistence of either *obsessions* or *compulsions*. Obsessions are ego-dystonic thoughts that are recurrent and persistent even when attempts are made to ignore them. Compulsions are comprised of activities or behaviors engaged in so that some effect is obtained or consequence is prevented, although no realistic causal relationship exists between the behavior and the construed event. Resistance to the compulsion results in increased tension, which dissipates after engaging in the compulsion. Obsessions and compulsions interfere with social, academic, and occupational functioning and cause the individual some distress. The condition is not attributable to another existing mental disorder such as Tourette's Disorder, Schizophrenia, Major Depression, or Organic Mental Disorder. It is distinguished from Disorders of Impulse Control Not Elsewhere Classified in that the nature of the activity itself provides some degree of pleasure or release in the latter case.

Onset is usually in adolescence or early adulthood, although it may occur more frequently in childhood than its estimated 1% occurrence in child psychiatric patients. Childhood cases closely resemble the adult clinical picture. Recovery rate is only about 50%, however, a fact that merits increased efforts on the part of clinicians to make early identification and initiate interventive treatment in understanding this chronic and incapacitating illness. Depressive symptoms are common, but case reports indicate that onset of depression usually occurs after onset of obsessive/compulsive symptoms. Both diagnoses should be used if diagnostic criteria are met.

Post-traumatic Stress Disorder. This category warrants a brief comment if only to stress the importance of differential diagnosis. This subtype is provided for reactions to situations of extreme stress and psychological trauma that are beyond the range of normal human experience. Symptoms of Anxiety, Depressive, and Organic Mental Disorders may also develop after excessive trauma and should be diagnosed according to their respective criteria. Adjustment Disorder would rarely involve a stressor of equal magnitude and the quality of reliving the trauma would be absent. Similarly, problems that might be coded under the V Codes (Uncomplicated Bereavement, Phase of Life Problem) may be described as traumatic stress but are within the range of everyday human experience.

Atypical Anxiety Disorder. This subtype is used for those instances of Anxiety Disorder that do not meet criteria for the other specified illnesses. Careful documentation and comparison with the other categories are the only way such a category will be helpful to future study of these disorders.

CASE VIGNETTE: ALEX

Alex is a 13-year-old boy referred by his psychiatrist for "compulsions." About six months ago, he began laying out his clothes and smoothing them for several minutes before putting them on; then he would open and close the dresser drawers. Three months later he began putting on and taking off his pants several times. A month ago he had to say where he was going eight times, after which his mother had to say "OK"; otherwise he would feel frustrated and repeat himself again. At school he opened and closed his locker door repeatedly. On arriving home, he had to enter and exit the house three or four times to touch his bicycle left outside. For the past five months, he has avoided stepping on sidewalk cracks. He has always been shy, but three or four months ago he stopped seeing his few friends.

Compulsion did not appear until this year. At age three, however, his parents had to say "Goodnight" 10 or 12 times before he could sleep. This need lasted a few months only. At age eight he told his mother he had a "radio" in his head. It told him to do good things in complete sentences and he enjoyed it. It lasted for a year and he wishes it "would come back."

About the same time his rituals started this year, his speech became quieter and murmuring. Three months ago he began to stop in midsentence, leaving out pronouns and prepositions. According to his mother, he can still speak in complete sentences when relaxed. He also blurts out irrelevant statements in class, although they may have been relevant to previously addressed subjects, and has episodes of unprovoked silly laughter or tearfulness, which he can't stop.

Medical examination revealed a mild-standing head tumor and some fidgetiness. The patient had been off thioridazine for a month. An EEG is described as abnormal with paroxysmal bursts of activity.

During the psychiatric interview the patient was cooperative; however, he repeatedly pulled on his upper lip and seemed to fidget. Affect was shallow, narrow, stable, and occasionally inappropriate. Mood was mostly apathetic. He occasionally smiled or giggled for no reason, but denied perceptual disturbances, delusions, or first-rank symptoms of Schneider. He was fully oriented. Concentration and intermediate memory were good. Speech was asyndetic and contained instances of blocking, derailment, and telegraphic speech perseveration, as well as delayed and immediate echolalia.

Diagnosis
   Axis I: 298.90 Atypical Psychosis
   Axis II: None
   Axis III: Possible Seizure Disorder
             Possible Tardive Dyskinesia
   Axis IV: None—1
   Axis V: Good—3

Discussion
Alex initially presented in a manner superficially resembling Obsessive Compulsive Disorder. However, the bizarre behavior and increasingly obvious thought disorder make the diagnosis of psychosis most apparent. It may be argued that Alex's condition is progressively advancing toward 295.1 Schizophrenia (Disorganized Type), but to the child psychiatrists seeing the patient early in the disorder, this is less apparent. The blocking and difficulty speaking suggest absence seizures to the neurologist and a trial of antiepileptic medication is being undertaken.

Chapter 14

Disorders Manifesting a Physical Nature

These disorders—Eating Disorders, Stereotyped Movement Disorders, and Other Disorders With Physical Manifestations—demonstrate fairly straightforward symptom patterns characterized by specific physical impairment.

EATING DISORDERS: DIAGNOSTIC CRITERIA

Eating Disorders: DSM-III Codes
307.10 Anorexia Nervosa
307.51 Bulimia
307.52 Pica
307.53 Rumination Disorder of Infancy
307.50 Atypical Eating Disorder

Each of the five subtypes of Eating Disorders are characterized by gross alterations in eating behavior. Of the five, Pica and Rumination usually occur during infancy and early childhood, while the others are typically adolescent phenomena. Rumination and Anorexia may progress to death.

Anorexia Nervosa

The essential feature of Anorexia Nervosa is an intense fear of becoming obese, accompanied by significant and excessive weight loss, which is not associated with any physical disorder. It most frequently occurs in females between the ages of 12 to 18 and is a relatively common diagnosis. Accompanying symptoms include disturbed body image, refusal to gain weight, and amenorrhea in females. The DSM-III criteria specify a weight loss of at least 25% of original body weight or, if under 18, 25% under expected weight as determined by growth charts.

The diagnosis is unlikely to present a problem, as weight loss in Major Depression is seldom as profound and is not associated with a fear of becoming fat. In Schizophrenia, atypical eating patterns may be evident, but other symptoms are seldom associated with anorexia. It is possible, however, for Anorexia Nervosa to be diagnosed together with Schizophrenia or Major Depression.

Bulimia

Bulimia is being recognized with increasing frequency. It is identified by episodic binge eating and preoccupation with this abnormal eating pattern. The individual may experience alternate periods of rabid craving and great concern over inability to stop overeating. There may be vomiting between episodes or laxative abuse. Depression and self-critical thoughts usually follow the binges. There is no evidence of a physical cause for the disorder. It should be differentiated from Anorexia Nervosa, as some anorexics also have bulimic episodes. In bulimia, however, there may be weight fluctuation and overemphasis on eating, but weight loss is never as severe as in anorexia.

Pica

Persistent consumption of non-nutritive substances such as dirt, plaster, hair, bugs, and/or pebbles characterizes this disorder. There is no aversion to food. Onset is usually between 12 and 24 months of age with remission in childhood; it rarely persists into adolescence or adulthood. The problem is more common in children who are poorly supervised or retarded. The DSM-III criteria specify that it is not due to another mental disorder, such as Infantile Autism or Schizophrenia, or to a physical disorder.

Rumination Disorder of Infancy

Rumination is a well-defined syndrome. Although it was first described in adult patients, it is much more common in children. The essential feature is repeated regurgitation of partially digested food, which is then chewed, spit out, or swallowed without nausea, retching, or other signs of gastrointestinal distress. The condition is potentially fatal because of weight loss or no weight gain and subsequent malnutrition. The infant may find that the process of bringing the food into the mouth is pleasurable. The disorder may begin at three to 12 months of age, though onset is later in retarded infants. Physical examination rules out possible physiological factors that may contribute to the symptoms.

CASE VIGNETTE: RICHARD THE SMELLY SMILER
Richard was admitted to the pediatric ward at eight months of age with principal complaint of failure to gain weight. His mother was also concerned about his persistent odor. Development had been normal up to the age of six months. During the subsequent months he had begun to display a peculiar behavior after each feeding. He would sit up, his head high and neck arched back, open his mouth until milk appeared, then either reswallow it or let it dribble down his chin. The milk seemed to be the source of Richard's very sour smell. The mother was unmarried, living with different relatives for periods at a time, which meant that Richard had been handed around to several different caretakers. Baby Richard, however, appeared content, smiled readily, and was reported to be easy to take care of.

Diagnosis
    Axis I: 307.53 Rumination Disorder of Infancy
    Axis II: None
    Axis III: None
    Axis IV: Moderate—4 (unwanted pregnancy)
    Axis V: Good (if applicable)—3

Discussion
Richard manifests all of the features of Rumination Disorder. He proved unusually difficult to feed however, as special caretaking, increased attention, and feeding with very thick cereal were not successful. He finally responded to adverse conditioning. Mild electric shocks were applied to his leg when he displayed ruminating behaviors. With one week of this treatment he stopped ruminating and was still well at one-year follow-up. Here, an Axis IV which named psychosocial stressors would be more informative.

CASE VIGNETTE: DEBORAH

Deborah, a 15-year-old who lives with her parents, asked to be seen because of binge eating and vomiting. Her weight ranged from 160 pounds when she was 14 to a low of 125. She has a tendency to be slightly chubby, as she is only 5'2".

At age 12 she started binge eating and vomiting; before that she always had a tendency to overeat. She is an excellent athlete, jogs six to eight miles a day, and plays competitive basketball at her high school.

She has periods when she feels depressed, mainly because of friction at home between her parents. She is more likely to binge during these times, eating in secret, usually junk food, but it can be anything available. At other times, however, the bingeing will start when things are relatively calm. She then becomes depressed about how fat she looks and refuses dates because of her embarrassment.

She is a good student and is very curious psychologically about the basis for her bingeing. She says she now understands how an alcoholic must feel (she has no interest in alcohol), because she knows the eating is bad for her but simply can't stop when she starts bingeing.

Diagnosis

   Axis I: 307.51 Bulimia
   Axis II: None
   Axis III: None
   Axis IV: Moderate—4 (hostile relationship between parents)
   Axis V: Good—3

Discussion

Deborah is typical of many bulimics with onset in adolescence, sometimes but not invariably associated with depressed mood. Enormous quantities of food are consumed, often secretly, with large fluctuation in body weight. It might be reasonable to add the diagnosis of Adjustment Disorder with Depressed Mood if the nature of the stressor were more extreme, but it would not add substantially since depression, at least mild depression, is usually associated with bulimia. Although bulimia can be associated with Anorexia Nervosa, there is no evidence of this here, as Deborah has never been thin. A diagnosis of Depression is not made in this case because depressive symptoms are not severe enough to interfere with overall functioning.

CASE VIGNETTE: ROGER

Roger, a two-year-old black male, has been brought to the clinic by his mother because of stomach pains. He has been slow to develop, sitting at one year of age and walking at 20 months. In addition, he is somewhat small for his age. During the many hours that Roger is left unattended in the family yard, he has been seen to pick up and eat dirt, sand, bugs and leaves. He often vomits these substances, but then resumes eating. He has had constipation and pain before.

During hospital admission, he received a lot of attention from the ward nurses because he was "cute and friendly." While in the hospital, he showed no tendency to eat non-nutritive substances. There was apprehension about returning him home, however, where the supervision was poor (by a mentally retarded grandmother who herself is said to eat plaster).

Diagnosis

   Axis I: 307.52 Pica
   Axis II: 319.0 Unspecified Mental Retardation
   Axis III: None
   Axis IV: Moderate (insufficient parental control)—4
   Axis V: Poor—5

Discussion

Bizarre eating patterns can occur with psychosis but Roger displays no evidence of this, nor does he fit the description of autism (friendly, language not specifically delayed). Pica is frequently associated with mental retardation, which is suspected because of the slow development. The lack of supervision and even the familial pattern are considered typical.

CASE VIGNETTE: KATHY

Kathy is a 15-year-old girl who was referred for an initial evaluation to an outpatient therapist because of preoccupation with exercise and weight loss. During the following six months, she went from her usual weight of 125 pounds to 80 pounds, at which point she was hospitalized. During hospitalization, she was irritable, denied having a problem, and volunteered for patient activities involving food, i.e., cooking for ward parties, etc. She was polite and superficially cooperative on the ward, although food intake had to be monitored carefully because of her ingenious ways of disposing of food. She was amenorrheic. During hospitalization, she was noted to have many obsessive ideas, such as feeling she must walk in a certain rhythm, and to feel compelled to follow routines. These interfered slightly with her recreational activities.

Her parents report that she was even-tempered, well behaved, and almost "too good" as a child. Before becoming ill, she had been a good student and had had a few close friends.

She was discharged at a weight of 95 pounds and has been stable at about 105 pounds in outpatient therapy.

Diagnosis
    Axis I: 307.10 Anorexia Nervosa
    Axis II: None
    Axis III: None
    Axis IV: None
    Axis V: Very good—2

Discussion
This is a typical picture of Anorexia Nervosa. There is seldom difficulty with this diagnosis because of the preoccupation with weight and profound weight loss in the absence of physical illness. The excessive exercise, interest in food, and compulsive traits are also commonly associated. The case is slightly unusual in the relative absence of associated depression, although she was irritable on the ward.

STEREOTYPED MOVEMENT DISORDERS: DIAGNOSTIC CRITERIA

Stereotyped Movement Disorders: DSM-III Codes
307.21 Transient Tic Disorder
307.22 Chronic Motor Tic Disorder
307.23 Tourette's Disorder
307.20 Atypical Tic Disorder
307.30 Atypical Stereotyped Movement Disorder

The presenting feature of Stereotyped Movement Disorders is an abnormality of gross motor movement. The disorder includes transient tics, chronic motor tics and Tourette's syndrome. Any association between the disorders is, as yet, unknown, but they may all be variations of one disorder.

Tics account for only approximately 5% of cases referred to child guidance clinics, but they have received considerable interest of late in terms of the amount of distress caused the child and the efficacy of drug treatment for Tourette's Disorder. Appearing primarily in the upper portion of the face, tics resemble patterns of startle response. They are defined as involuntary and rapid movement of a group of functionally related skeletal muscles or involuntary production of sounds or words. These characteristics distinguish tics from other involuntary movement disorders: choreiform, dystonic, athetoid, and myoclonic movements as well as other more rare neurological conditions such as hemiballismus. Spasms are differentiated by slower, more prolonged disturbance involving groups of muscles. Tics must also be distinguished from dyskinesias, which are silent oral-buccal-lingual movements and limb movements.

Movement disorders arise most commonly in early childhood, with average age of onset at seven years, and only rarely in adolescence. They are more common in males of average or above average intelligence, a factor contributing to diagnostic distinction from stereotypies of the mentally retarded. Both emotional and hysterical qualities have been cited as possible precipitating factors; however, few emotional causes have been linked to these disorders. While stress may act to exacerbate tics, occurrence during tranquil periods of life is just as typical of the symptom course. A minority of cases does support association with symptoms of emotional disturbance, for example, anxiety; there are, however, few instances of association with behavior disorders. Attention Deficit Disorder, on the other hand, is a frequent presenting problem or associated condition with Tourette's syndrome. Familial patterns have also been reported for all forms of Stereotyped Movement Disorders, although nonfamilial cases are most commonly encountered. Evidence of nervous system "immaturity" or early pre- and perinatal insult has been documented, but the association is not striking.

Accompanying features often include considerable self-consciousness and secondary symptoms of depression. Both social and academic functioning may suffer as a result of the severity of the tic in combination with self-consciousness on the part of the patient and those interacting with him or her.

Transient Tic Disorder
Transient Tic Disorder must have its onset during early childhood or adolescence; cases have been reported as early as two years of age. The re-

currence of the involuntary tics can be voluntarily suppressed for a period of time up to several hours. The intensity of the symptoms can vary over a period of weeks or months, but the criteria for the transient disorder require duration for at least one month but not more than one year. Eye blinks or other facial tics are most common, but limbs or torso may also be involved. The tics may disappear but typically recur and worsen during periods of stress. Transient tics are common and may occur in 10–20% of school-aged children. Differential diagnosis is evaluated in terms of chronicity, or development of Tourette's Disorder, involving vocal tics.

Chronic Motor Tic Disorder
Chronic Motor Tic Disorder is very similar to Transient Tic Disorder, with the exception that the intensity of symptoms is constant over weeks or months and duration exceeds one year. Vocal tics are unusual and, if persistent, would indicate Tourette's Disorder.

Chronic tics usually begin in childhood or after age 40, have a chronic course, and tend to be limited to no more than three particular muscle groups. They are also thought to be more common in males.

Transient Tic Disorder differs from Chronic Motor Tic Disorder in intensity and duration of the disturbance, while in Tourette's Disorder intensity may vary over time, vocal tics are much more prominent, and motor movements tend to be brief and weak as compared to those in Chronic Motor Tic Disorder.

Tourette's Disorder
The essential features once again involve involuntary repetitive motor movements, but these must be accompanied by multiple vocal tics. Motor tics involve the head and may include other parts of the body as well, particularly torso and upper limbs. Vocal tics include various sounds, such as grunts, yelps, sniffs, coughs, or words. Coprolalia, the involuntary uttering of obscenities, is present in 60% of the cases. Tics may be voluntarily suppressed for minutes or hours and vary in intensity. Duration of more than one year is required for diagnosis.

Associated features include imitation of observed motions (echokinesis), repeating what one has just said (palilalia), mental coprolalia, obsessive thoughts, compulsions to touch things or impulsive performance of complicated movements. The disorder may appear by age two and is almost always present by age 13; diagnostic criteria indicate a cutoff age of 15 years. It is three times more common in boys than in girls and occurrence among family members is more frequent than in the general population.

Atypical Tic Disorder
This category is for tics that do not meet the criteria for classification in the previous categories.

Atypical Stereotyped Movement Disorder
The category is indicated for conditions involving voluntary and nonspasmodic movement which may or may not have associated distress accompanying the symptoms. Such conditions are found almost exclusively in children and may include head-banging, repetitive hand movement, or rocking. Incidence is especially prevalent in children with Mental Retardation and Pervasive Developmental Disorder, is common in those lacking adequate social stimulation, and may also occur in absence of mental disorder.

CASE VIGNETTE: DAVID
Nine-year-old David had been receiving outpatient treatment at a child guidance clinic for two years because of hyperactive, inattentive, and immature behavior. For about a year he had been tried on stimulant medication, which was helpful in controlling his behavior. However, while on stimulants he began to develop facial tics and had throat clearing. The tics continued even when stimulants were discontinued. The throat clearing had originally been ascribed to allergy; however, it progressed over the following year to grunts, and the facial tics were eventually accompanied by jerks of the shoulder.

Diagnosis
    Axis I: 307.23 Tourette's Disorder (Multiple verbal/motor tic disorder)
    Axis II: None
    Axis III: None
    Axis IV: Unspecified—0
    Axis V: Fair—4

Discussion
This patient's history is typical of that of about 50% of males with Tourette's Disorder, including a prior diagnosis or symptom pattern of Attention Deficit Disorder with Hyperactivity. The role of stimulants in the onset of this disorder is not clear; however, for at least some patients this type of medication seems to aggravate, if not initiate, the syndrome. A diagnosis of ADD would not be made in this case, although for many patients

with Tourette's, the restless and inattentive behavior of ADD may be the most difficult aspect of the patient's condition.

OTHER DISORDERS WITH PHYSICAL MANIFESTATIONS: DIAGNOSTIC CRITERIA

Other Disorders With Physical Manifestations: DSM-III Codes
307.00 Stuttering 307.60 Functional Enuresis 307.70 Functional Encopresis 307.46 Sleepwalking Disorder 307.46 Sleep Terror Disorder (307.49)

These disorders affect physical functioning in the areas of speech, excretion, and sleep. Psychological conflict was formerly thought to be the cause of these conditions; however, few children with these specific disorders have associated mental disturbance.

Stuttering
Stuttering or stammering is characterized by prolonged repetition of sounds and syllables, abnormal hesitations and pauses, all of which disrupt normal speech rhythms. There may be accompanying jerks, blinks, and tremors; extent of the disturbance typically varies by situation. Onset is usually before age 12 and course is often chronic with periods of remission. In milder cases, over 50% recovery is reported.

Functional Enuresis
Diagnostic indications are a continued pattern of involuntary voiding of urine not accounted for by physical disorder and occurring after the age at which continence is expected. If bladder control has not been established prior to onset, the disorder is called *primary*; otherwise, onset after a one-year period of continence is referred to as *secondary*. No means for coding this distinction has been provided. An age criterion specifies that in five- and six-year-olds occurrence is two times per month and in older children it is once a month. Functional Encopresis, Sleepwalking Disor-

der, and Sleep Terror Disorder are also reported as accompanying complaints.

Functional Encopresis
In this disorder the distinction between *primary* and *secondary* occurrence is also made, but no code is specified. Its prominent characteristic is the voluntary or involuntary passage of feces in places that are inappropriate for the social and cultural background of the child. The involuntary/voluntary distinction is associated with contributing factors, such as constipation or retention in the case of involuntary passage of feces. Antisocial or psychopathological processes may be behind deliberate incontinence. Physical disorder must be ruled out for the diagnosis.

Sleepwalking Disorder and Sleep Terror Disorder
Sleepwalking Disorder is diagnosed on report of repeated episodes when the individual rises from bed and walks about. He/she is nonresponsive to others during this time and later has no recollection of the event. At the time of occurrence, it is nearly impossible to rouse the individual. After awakening, there is no evidence of impaired mental activity or of behavior, though a brief period of confusion or disorientation may initially ensue. There is no evidence of abnormal brain activity during sleep or that the episode occurs specifically during REM sleep.

Sleep Terror Disorder is described as a pattern of incidents typified by abrupt awakening, usually preceded by a panicky scream, with evidence of intense anxiety apparent throughout the episode. There is relative unresponsiveness to others during the occurrence, at which time the person appears confused and disoriented and exhibits, at times, perseverative motions. No evidence of abnormal brain activity or REM sleep is linked to the episode.

There is no association between these disturbances and any other mental disorder. Epileptic seizure activity would rule out these diagnoses. Sleep Terror Disorder has a different quality than nightmares, in which the anxiety experience is milder and the person is able to recall most or all portions of the dream sequence.

Chapter 15

Other Disorders of Infancy, Childhood, or Adolescence

This section of DSM-III is a catch-all for those disturbances of an emotional nature that were not included in DSM-II. We have found, however, that some of the disorders are suited to placement beside other major categories for convenience of discussion or to point out diagnostic differences. Reactive Attachment Disorder of Infancy found a niche in the discussion of Pervasive Developmental Disorder (Chapter 9); Schizoid Disorder of Childhood and Adolescence was inserted next to Schizophrenia (Chapter 10); and Oppositional Disorder was placed alongside Attention Deficit Disorder and Conduct Disorder (Chapter 12). The remaining disturbances to be discussed here include Elective Mutism and Identity Disorder. We have also taken the liberty of briefly commenting on Childhood Gender Disturbances and Adjustment Disorder.

DSM-III Codes
313.23 Elective Mutism
313.82 Identity Disorder
302.60 Gender Identity Disorder of Childhood
309.xx Types of Adjustment Disorder

ELECTIVE MUTISM

The essential aspect in Elective Mutism is refusal to speak in almost all situations, despite adequate speech and language development and comprehension. This type of child may at times communicate through gestures and other nonverbal communication. The refusal to speak is not due to another mental disorder or to any developmental disability, even though there is reported incidence of delayed language development or articulation difficulties.

Associated behavioral disturbance is often observed, particularly negativism and oppositional behavior. The disorder usually comes to the attention of school personnel initially, as mutism can lead to academic underachievement or failure and social ostracism. What little research there is points to continued behavioral difficulties, even when speech is resumed.

Differential diagnoses are Severe or Profound Mental Retardation, Pervasive Developmental Disorder, or Developmental Language Disorder. A general refusal to speak may also be apparent in cases of Major Depression, Avoidant Disorder of Childhood or Adolescence, Overanxious Disorder, Oppositional Disorder, and Social Phobia. None of these disorders manifests a prominent lack of speech, however, and intellectual testing and general psychiatric evaluation will quickly point out these distinctions. Excessively shy children or children from families who speak a different language from that of the dominant culture may also present with speech refusal.

IDENTITY DISORDER

The debilitating feature of this disorder is succinctly summarized by the question, "Who am I?" Identity Disorder originates in the subject's inability to reconcile a variety of issues and integrate a coherent and acceptable sense of self. As a result, academic, social, and occupational functioning is impaired, with varying degree of severity, for a period of more than three months. Onset typically occurs in late adolescence.

Differential consideration evaluates the degree to which the conflict deviates from the normal process of maturing and separation from the family constellation. Severity of the distress and ensuing impairment offer guidelines for determining deviation from a normal developmental process. Diagnosis of Schizophrenia, Schizophreniform Disorder, or Affective Disorder preempts consideration of Identity Disorder as a diagnosis.

Borderline Personality Disorder is considered if the patient is over age 18; however, its particular characteristics involve several areas of impairment, and disturbance of mood is prominent. In such cases, when these latter criteria are met, this diagnosis would be used in place of Identity Disorder.

There is an uncertain relationship between incidence of Identity Disorder in adolescence and appearance of more severe forms of mental disorder later in life.

GENDER IDENTITY DISORDER OF CHILDHOOD

Disorders of this type are typified by incongruence between gender identity and anatomic sex. Definition of "gender identity" is related to public expression of gender role, which in turn is influenced by individual perception of gender.

In this particular childhood gender disturbance, symptoms are characterized by a persistent discomfort with anatomic sex and the desire to be, or insistence that one is, of the opposite sex.

The diagnostic criteria require strong evidence of this desire to be of the opposite sex. Repeated repudiation of the given anatomic sexual structures is accepted as evidence if onset is prior to puberty.

Age of onset is often early; for example, in males, 75% of reported cases began cross-dressing before age four; however, the disorder rarely presents in mental health clinics until the child reaches puberty. Exposure to social conflict often results in repression of the behaviors during late childhood. There is an undetermined association with homosexual patterns in adolescence or later adult life; a relatively infrequent association with transsexualism has also been seen. These adult disorders also often have onset in childhood. Occurrence of any other major disorder is rare, though there may be phobias or persistent nightmares in some instances. Social impairment varies in relation to the degree of reaction by family and peers.

ADJUSTMENT DISORDER

Adjustment Disorder is not placed under the Childhood Disorder section of DSM-III; however, because this diagnosis is used to a considerable extent by child psychiatrists, it is discussed here.

The essential feature of Adjustment Disorder is that there is a maladaptive reaction that occurs *within three months* of the onset of a stressor.

Such stressors may include changing schools, parental separation, or illness in the family. In terms of severity Adjustment Disorders fall in between V Code conditions, where there is no maladaptive behavior, and the more severe disorders. For example, if criteria for Depression or Conduct Disorder are fulfilled, then Adjustment Disorder should not be used. One of the advantages of a multiaxial scheme is that Axis I is for description alone, and Axis IV can be used to record psychosocial stressors. Therefore, if the criteria for a major disorder are met, there are still ways of recording the pertinent stressor. Since both the pattern of maladaptive behavior and the stressor have been recorded, different patterns of behavioral reaction can be compared on follow-up.

CASE VIGNETTE: SALLY

Six-year old Sally was referred by her kindergarten teacher to the local child guidance clinic because she would not speak during school. She had initially been very tearful and reluctant to have her mother leave her alone in school. Sally's mother said she had been periodically "obstinate" at home but without major problems. After a few weeks, however, she seemed to become accustomed to the school routine but gradually stopped talking. It was clear from the initial contact and from her nonverbal cooperation that her comprehension and speech development were at age level.

During the beginning of school, the patient's parents separated and mother became depressed. Home life was comfortable but both parents were rather uninvolved with the patient and with her younger sister. It was hard to find out if there had been much change in speech at home, but the younger sister reported that the patient still spoke with her.

Diagnosis

Axis I: 313.23 Elective Mutism
Axis II: None
Axis III: None
Axis IV: Mild—3
Axis V: Fair–poor—4–5

Discussion

This patient is typical of elective mutism, in that, in spite of the disturbed home situation, no other diagnosable mental disorder is apparent. The extent of true mutism at home is hard to ascertain, but the continuation of speech with at least a sibling is typical.

CASE VIGNETTE: CHARLES

Charles, a 14-year-old boy whose parents had been divorced since he was eight, was evaluated because in the past two months he had been breaking a variety of school rules and fighting with other children, unlike his previous behavior. This had started after his return from summer vacation. Charles has always had difficulty with reading, and is in a special reading program in his junior high school.

He had been in California with his father for the summer. Unlike previous summers, which had been mutually enjoyable, this year his father's time had been monopolized by a girlfriend whom the father planned to marry. She resented Charles's presence and arranged for him to be with children he didn't know so she could spend time with the father alone. Charles's mother was upset because the father was trying to reduce child support in connection with his forthcoming marriage.

When interviewed, the boy was friendly toward the examiner, but brash in criticizing the school rules and pointing out what "saps" his friends were. His boasts of being "cool" were out of proportion to any of his true offenses. He said he didn't think he wanted to continue school, but was very receptive to the interviewer's interest in and concern about his future. Psychological testing indicates bright normal intelligence, but reading is two years below grade level.

Diagnosis

Axis I: 309.30 Adjustment Disorder with Disturbance of Conduct
Axis II: 315.00 Developmental Reading Disorder
Axis III: None
Axis IV: Moderate (loss of nuclear family)—4
Axis V: Good—3

Discussion

This boy does not have sufficiently disturbed behavior to meet criteria for Conduct Disorder. His maladaptive behavior, beginning after his visit in the summer, makes Adjustment Disorder more appropriate than a V Code. In this case, an Axis IV code identifying the stressor would also be appropriate and most informative.

Chapter 16

Use of V Codes in Absence of Axis I or II Diagnosis

DSM-III has adapted from ICD-9-CM (International Classification of Diseases—Clinical Modification) a partial list of conditions that are the focus of clinical attention but are not attributable to mental disorder. This indicates that although the condition does not fit the DSM-III definition of "mental disorder," it is serious enough to merit attention and treatment. V Codes may also indicate absence of mental disorder or inadequate evaluation for determination of presence or absence of disorder. Unfortunately, they may not be coded in addition to another Axis I disorder. This is regrettable because the present Axis IV codes only severity of psychosocial stressor, although for child psychiatry the specific features found in V codes may be extremely important even when an Axis I disorder is present.

Many of the V Codes are particularly relevant to clinical work with children and families, and clinicians should be aware of their existence and make an effort to use them when applicable. This is, of course, especially appropriate for the instances in which a family or parent problem is the true focus of a child's presenting complaint rather than a disorder within the child.

There may be some redundancy when V Codes and Axis IV factors are both coded; however, V Codes are used in place of an Axis I diagnosis when the presence of the condition initiates contact with the diagnosing agency. Axis IV is used to provide additional information when a disorder is present and, as it now stands, stresses severity rather than the specific

118

stressors. V Codes presently indicate the presence of a condition requiring treatment in the absence of any other relevant Axis I disorder.

V Codes
V62.89 Borderline Intellectual Functioning
V71.02 Childhood or Adolescent Antisocial Behavior
V62.30 Academic Problem
V61.20 Parent-Child Problem
V61.80 Other Specified Family Circumstances
V61.10 Marital Problem
V7   No Diagnosis

BORDERLINE INTELLECTUAL FUNCTIONING

This diagnosis is used when the focus of attention or treatment is associated with Borderline Intellectual Functioning, i.e., an IQ between 71 and 84. The diagnosis of Borderline Intellectual Functioning is particularly problematic for children in the presence of social and educational deprivation. However, there are many school consultations which arise simply because of the discrepancy between the intellectual level of the child and the surrounding demands of certain school systems. Here this code might be useful even when an Axis I disorder *is* present.

CHILD OR ADOLESCENT ANTISOCIAL BEHAVIOR

This is used for isolated antisocial acts, not apparently due to another disorder such as Conduct Disorder or Adjustment Disorder with Disturbance of Conduct.

ACADEMIC PROBLEM

There is a pattern of failing grades or significant underachievement in the absence of specific developmental disorder or other mental disorder.

PARENT-CHILD PROBLEM

This category can be used when focus of attention is a parent-child problem not due to another apparent mental disorder. An example is child abuse, not attributable to mental disorder in the parent.

OTHER SPECIFIED FAMILY CIRCUMSTANCES

Examples are difficulties with an aged relative or sibling rivalry.

MARITAL PROBLEM

Marital conflict related to divorce, estrangement, or separation custody disputes can cause distress for a child otherwise without mental disorder. The primary disturbance would not be attributable to the child being evaluated, but to his/her circumstances. The marital difficulty is not due to mental disorder or the part of those involved.

NO DIAGNOSIS

This can be used in place of either Axis I or Axis II.

CASE VIGNETTE: MATTHEW

Seven-year-old Matthew is brought to the clinic by his stepfather, who complains that he is "too effeminate" and that there "must be something wrong with him." The stepfather complains that the boy is too mild and shows no interest in sports. Mother feels there is nothing wrong with her son, but thinks stepfather is envious of her close relationship with Matthew and upset that they have had no children together. On interview, the boy is somewhat shy, prefers quiet play, but has no other difficulties. His teacher says he functions well in school.

Diagnosis
    Axis I: None
            V Code 61.20 or 61.80 (see Discussion)
    Axis II: None
    Axis III: None
    Axis IV: Moderate (rejection by stepfather)—4
    Axis V: Good—3

Discussion
This could be coded under Parent-Child Problem or Other Specified Family Circumstances (V61.20 or V61.80). Such coding provides a record of the contact, but does not attribute a mental disorder to the child when in fact none has been determined.

Chapter 17

Axis II: Specific Developmental Disorders

The multiaxial approach of DSM-III makes it possible to describe disturbance and accompanying features of disorder more completely than any other approach to date. These Axis II disorders delineate specific or otherwise noted deviations from usual development associated with learning and language that are not attributed to another mental disorder. That these difficulties are included within a classification of mental disorders has raised eyebrows. Objections usually center on the facts that psychopathology is not involved, that diagnostic and treatment functions are usually performed within the educational system, and that such children are stigmatized by inclusion in this classification. Despite lack of resolution of these issues, many instances of Specific Developmental Disorder requiring treatment have been cited along with some of the Axis I disorders. Coding of the Axis II disorders in the future will ensure that they are not neglected and may shed some light on their interesting partnership with Attention Deficit Disorder and Conduct Disorder. It is also important to note that in many cases Specific Developmental Disorders are coded on Axis II, but Axis I has "no mental disorder."

Because their occurrence is so common, Specific Developmental Disorders should be routinely considered as part of diagnostic differentiation in all cases of developmental delay, school failure, and behavior problems in school or elsewhere. The exact specifications for "significant" delay and the ability to detect Specific Developmental Disorder will vary with age. The disorder is not simply a deficit in biological maturation; in fact, evidence of the difficulty, in most cases, is still apparent in adulthood. In rare cases, the symptoms may improve over time; however, clinically significant symptoms in adolescence or adulthood should be noted.

EVALUATION AND DIFFERENTIATION

The major diagnostic groups which are differentiated in all cases are Mental Retardation, visual and auditory sensory impairments, and Pervasive Developmental Disorders. Occasionally, in instances of Mild to Moderate Mental Retardation, a Specific Developmental Disorder can coexist. This determination requires careful testing and evaluation, and familiarity with achievement levels within the retarded range. All diagnoses in this category rely heavily on the results of intellectual, speech, and hearing testing.

DSM-III is relatively clear about the criteria for these disorders, and they will not be repeated here. One slight flaw is that significant degree of disorder is not spelled out nor is any consideration given to age variation in degree of developmental lag. It is important to realize, therefore, the significance that clinical experience plays in accurately recognizing manifestations of these difficulties. For example, if grade level is used to determine degree of impairment, should achievement be one or two years behind grade level? This criterion would not be too helpful for preschool and early elementary years, a period in which diagnosis and remediation may have a crucial impact on future outcome. Similarly, correction for IQ is important, particularly for children with low-normal intelligence and for those in affluent educational school systems.

Specific Developmental Disorders: DSM-III Codes

315.00 Developmental Reading Disorder
315.10 Developmental Arithmetic Disorder
315.31 Developmental Language Disorder
       Receptive Type (no separate code)
       Expressive Type (no separate code)
315.39 Developmental Articulation Disorder
315.50 Mixed Specific Developmental Disorder
315.90 Atypical Specific Developmental Disorder

It is worth noting that there are several more categories than previously included in DSM-II. Articulation Disorder has been purposely separated from Language Disorder and the receptive and expressive subtypes of Language Disorder have been distinguished, though fifth digit coding is not available.

CASE VIGNETTE: CARL

Carl, seven years old, is brought to the clinic at the request of his school psychologist because of difficulty with schoolwork and restless behavior in class. Carl is seen as immature and often does not appear to listen when the teacher gives instructions. He has always had poor coordination.

The parents, both high school graduates, have had no complaints about Carl up to this time, although mother thinks Carl was somewhat slow in starting to talk and to speak in full sentences.

Examination in the clinic shows a friendly, cooperative child who is mildly restless during the examination. Psycholinguistic testing indicates immature language development in spite of good ability to understand instructions. Carl's spoken language is clear but immature, and he uses relatively simple and concrete phrases. Reading ability is also below age level. Full Scale IQ is 90; Verbal 80; Performance 105.

Diagnosis

Axis I: Possible Attention Deficit Disorder—mild
Axis II: 315.31 Developmental Language Disorder,
  Expressive Type
Axis III: None
Axis IV: No information—0
Axis V: Fair—4

Discussion

Without psychological testing, Carl could be misdiagnosed as a "simple case" of Attention Deficit Disorder. The more important remediation here is educational and psycholinguistic. Moreover, without attention to the differential diagnosis of reading difficulty, the basis for the reading problem would go undetected. A diagnosis of Developmental Reading Disorder is premature in this case.

Epidemiological data show a powerful association between the developmental language disorders and a variety of Axis I syndromes. Carl's case is typical, as at least half of the children with developmental language disorders exhibit some behavioral disturbance. The mechanisms mediating this relationship are not understood.

Section IV

Looking Ahead

Chapter 18

Conclusions

> **WARNING:** DSM-III may be hazardous to your good sense! Application of DSM-III criteria is not prescribed without prior and extensive clinical experience.

DSM-III seems clear in its criteria and in its descriptive, atheoretical approach. This may lead to a false sense of security in practicing diagnostics. The most difficult part of the diagnostic process is recognizing the specific behaviors and the degree of impairment that they may represent. Usually, an extensive combination of clinical training and experience is required to attain the degree of expertise needed to apply a diagnostic system. Intensive exposure to children with specific handicaps and specific behavioral disturbances at all ages—from infancy to early adulthood for childhood disorders—is essential for mastery of diagnosis.

At a recent Board Examination for Child Psychiatry, one of the authors was struck by the frequency with which an "exam case," a five-year-old deaf child, was diagnosed as *autistic*. The examinees knew the DSM-III criteria for autism perfectly; however, they incorrectly evaluated the behaviors of the child shown on the videotape, interpreting dance steps as "abnormal stereotyped movements" and sign language between child and teacher simply as the "absence of speech associated with autism." Improved clarity within the diagnostic classification system cannot address this kind of ignorance!

Development of diagnostic sense in child psychiatry and other disciplines must involve hundreds of hours of exposure to normal and abnormal children with a wide variety of symptom patterns. It is beyond the scope of this book to outline clinical training for child psychiatry, except to stress the desirability of supervision in which senior supervisors also have direct contact with the case through tapes, sitting in on or observing the interview, or through an additional independent interview. Clear descriptive labels are actually the second step in the success of DSM-III. The first step must be to know what you are seeing.

ON TO DSM-IV
The APA DSM is continually under reexamination and revision. A task force has been assembled by the APA to make recommendations for revisions of DSM-III. Information from the "consumers" balanced with research evidence will, in fact, be the making of DSM-IV.

It is likely that an interim report (possibly titled DSM III-R) will follow many of the suggestions already proposed in this guide. There seems to be general dissatisfaction, for example, with Mental Retardation as an Axis I disorder and it is likely that it will find an axis of its own. There is also evidence from unpublished research that "pure" ADD can become Conduct Disorder and that the distinction between those two disorders may be overdone. Oppositional Disorder (which has been much opposed!) may predict a *variety* of problems in later childhood, cutting across broad categories of disorder. We hope Axis IV will be made more useful to child clinicians by stressing specific social situations.

Ideally, research studies and validating replications should be the basis for the changes. With the small research force within child psychiatry, the changes are likely to be small. Furthermore, DSM-IV (to appear around 1990) needs to remain compatible with ICD-10, and therefore will be under considerable constraint to minimize departures from that system. It is likely, however, that ICD-10 will become multiaxial, and thus the remaining differences will be more suitable. The major issues, of course, are the Axis I disorders: Are they valid? Do we have too many?

VALIDITY OF AXIS I DISORDERS AND
MULTIPLICITY OF DIAGNOSES
We see an important agenda for DSM-III within child psychiatry. This encompasses validation of several Axis I entities and probable alteration of some of the Axis II diagnoses as well. Since DSM-III urges multiple diag-

noses, it will undoubtedly influence clinicians, to a greater degree than did DSM-II, to list more individual diagnoses per patient. This is where the work comes in—making sense of these tabulations. Critics are concerned that this approach has already gotten out of hand; however, future DSM task forces will have to consider the relative merits of multiple diagnoses, compared with differential diagnosis, in the areas where validity of the distinctions is, as yet, unproven.

Axis I probably has more disorders defined than it should. The splitting of Conduct Disorder and Attention Deficit Disorder into subtypes may not be justified. The status of Oppositional Disorder has to be clarified as well. Is it a precursor to other disorders—depression, conduct, personality disorders or all of them? Is it a normal phase or a disorder in its own right? The application and appropriateness of DSM-III categories in the preschool age also deserve a great deal more attention and data!

USE OF AXES II, IV, AND V FOR CHILDHOOD DIAGNOSIS

As indicated in an earlier discussion (Chapter 3), we would recommend that DSM-IV adopt the British ICD-9 coding of intelligence on a separate axis. This would ensure assessment, provide consistent recording, and might increase the usefulness of Axis IV, at least within child psychiatry.

For children, unlike adults, personality disturbances are coded on Axis I. Insufficient information within the DSM text makes it unclear as to which adult personality disorders (Axis II) should be made before or only after age 18. This raises some important legitimate questions: first of all, can reliable diagnosis of personality disorder be made in children or adolescents? And second, are Axis I childhood personality disturbances actually continuous with Axis II adult versions? In practice, diagnoses such as Borderline and Narcissistic Personality Disorders are frequently made in adolescents. It is disconcerting, however, that structured interviews for children and adolescents with widespread use for research and epidemiological purposes do not contain research definitions of these disorders specific to this age group. Therefore, the extent to which they, as defined in DSM-III, occur as primary or secondary diagnoses is unknown. It also remains to be seen whether or not Identity Disorder has features in common with Borderline Personality Disorder in adulthood.

The Axis V designation by the British version of ICD-9 is keyed to psychosocial evaluation and specifies that abnormal social circumstances be coded if they are pertinent to diagnosis. As we have stressed repeatedly, the specific situation rather than its severity would seem to give more useful information for the purposes of understanding the case more fully and planning research. We suggest, at least within the childhood and adolescence section, that the international Axis V replace the existing DSM-III Axis IV, with one important exception: that no judgment relating causality between situation and behavior be made. The coding should simply indicate presence or absence of each particular circumstance. It is likely that DSM-III's Axis IV will be changed, as there is considerable general dissatisfaction with this axis.

Once again we extend a cautionary note concerning the clinical application of the diagnostic system. Use of DSM-III can only reflect the clinician's ability to correctly identify patient symptoms. Awareness of the differing limitations in collecting useful data extends beyond the hindrances of the classification system to the degree of error in recognizing behaviors. DSM-III is not a surrogate for experience; however, in proper hands it will be a powerful aid in the advancement of knowledge.

The opportunity for systematic observation and clear documentation and communication should prove useful to the private practitioner interested in collecting data for follow-up assessment in relation to treatment or naturalistic course. Commentary on the diagnostic gray areas in light of this kind of meticulous application will expedite future revisions and provide invaluable input for diagnostic understanding of childhood disorders.

Appendices

Appendix I

DSM-III and ICD-9 for Disorders First Arising in Childhood or Adolescence

Critics of DSM-III from abroad are concerned about its departure from ICD-9 and the nomenclature developed by the World Health Organization (WHO) for classification of disease, although DSM-III was designed and coded to be as comparable to ICD-9 as possible. (It should be noted that ICD-9 terminology is also acceptable to most U.S. hospitals and to most third-party payers.) The reasons for the departure, according to the DSM-III drafters, were:

> (1) It seemed that a system more particularly suitable for the U.S. was needed.
> (2) The use of more subtypes was considered desirable in many areas, and was supported by some current research.
> (3) Both operational criteria and a multiaxial approach were desired.

Because ICD-9 is used throughout the world, a brief discussion of some of the categories for children and adolescents is included to help child psychiatrists understand possible sources of diagnostic variation between Europe (particularly the U.K.) and the U.S. that are in part attributable to the different systems.

At the outset, let us address some confusion which exists regarding the use of the term "ICD-9." In fact, there are three versions:

(1) ICD-9 is the WHO version. It is not multiaxial, but has a second code within the section on psychiatric disorders to indicate medical codes for certain categories.
(2) ICD-9-CM is the clinical addition adapted by APA in which a fifth digit code was added to specify DSM-III terms and classification. See Appendix D of DSM-III.
(3) The U.K. version of ICD-9, developed primarily by Rutter, is multiaxial but has not been adopted by WHO (see DSM-III, pp. 405–406).

ICD-9, as used in England (Rutter et al., 1975), has some features in common with DSM-III, namely a multiaxial format, parts of which are included below.

ICD-9 MULTIAXIAL CLASSIFICATION OF PSYCHIATRIC DISORDERS*

AXIS ONE (Clinical Psychiatric Syndrome) PSYCHOSES (290–299)
Code 290   Senile and Presenile Organic Psychotic Conditions
    291   Alcoholic Psychoses
    292   Drug Induced Psychoses
    293   Transient Organic Psychotic Conditions
    294   Other Organic Psychotic Conditions (Chronic)
    295   Schizophrenic Psychoses
    296   Affective Psychoses
    297   Paranoid States
    298   Other Non-organic Psychoses
    299   Psychoses Specific to Childhood
NEUROTIC DISORDERS, PERSONALITY DISORDERS AND OTHER NON-PSYCHOTIC MENTAL DISORDERS (300–316)
Code 300   Personality or Character Disorders
    302   Sexual Deviations and Disorders
    303   Alcohol Dependence

---

*From: *A Guide to a Multi-axial Classification Scheme for Psychiatric Disorders in Childhood and Adolescence.* Prepared by M. L. Rutter, D. Shaffer, and C. Sturge. Department of Child and Adolescent Psychiatry, Institute of Psychiatry, De Crespigny Park, London SE5 A8AF, England.

304 Drug Dependence
305 Non-Dependent Abuse of Drugs
306 Physical Conditions Arising from Mental Factors
307 **Special Symptoms or Syndromes not Elsewhere Classified**
308 Acute Reaction to Stress
309 **Adjustment Reaction**
310 Specific Non-Psychotic Mental Disorders Following Organic Brain Damage
311 Depressive Disorders not Elsewhere Classified
312 **Disturbances of Conduct not Elsewhere Classified**
313 **Disturbances of Emotions Specific to Childhood and Adolescence**
314 **Hyperkinetic Syndrome of Childhood**
316 Psychic Factors Associated with Diseases Classified Elsewhere

AXIS TWO (Specific Delays in Development)
Code 0 No Specific Delay
      1 Specific Reading Retardation
      2 Specific Arithmetical Retardation
      3 Other Specific Learning Difficulties
      4 Developmental Speech/Language Disorder
      5 Specific Motor Retardation
      6 Mixed Developmental Disorder
      8 Other Specified
      9 Unspecified

AXIS THREE (Intellectual Level)
Code 0 Normal Variation
      1 Mild Mental Retardation
      2 Moderate Mental Retardation
      3 Severe Mental Retardation
      4 Profound Mental Retardation
      5 Unspecified Mental Retardation
      9 Intellectual Level Unknown

(AXIS FOUR (Medical Conditions)   see ICD-9)
AXIS FIVE (Associated Abnormal Psychosocial Situations)
      00 No significant distortion or inadequacy of psychosocial environment
      01 Mental disturbance in other family members
      02 Discordant intra-familial relationships
      03 Lack of warmth in intra-familial relationships

04 Familial over-involvement
05 Inadequate or inconsistent parental control
06 Inadequate social, linguistic or perceptual stimulation
07 Inadequate living conditions
08 Inadequate or distorted intra-familial communication
09 Anomalous family situation
10 Stresses or disturbance in school or work environment
11 Migration or social transplantation
12 Natural disaster
13 Other intra-familial psychosocial stress
14 Other extra-familial psychosocial stress
15 Persecution or adverse discrimination
16 Other psychosocial disturbance in society in general
88 Other (Specified)
99 Psychosocial Situation Unknown

The ICD-9/U.K. multiaxial system, Axes I, II, III, and V, differs in some respects from DSM-III. (Note that the ICD-9 multiaxial system is in use in the U.K. but is not an official part of the WHO system at this time.) The basic differences are:

(1) In ICD-9/U.K., intellectual functioning is coded on a separate axis, Axis III. At one time it was considered a possible ''substitute'' for DSM-III Axis V, Highest Level of Adaptive Functioning, which is not coded in the ICD-9/U.K. system. These ICD Axis III codings are similar to DSM-III codings for Mental Retardation on Axis I.
(2) Instead of coding severity of psychosocial stressor as in DSM-III (Axis IV), ICD-9/U.K. notes the current presence or absence of a particular stressor by code number (Axis V).
(3) Like DSM-III, developmental delays are placed on a separate ICD-9/U.K. axis (Axis II). Note that specific motor retardation (Clumsiness Syndrome) is present in ICD-9, but is not included in DSM-III, Axis II.

Readers interested in European literature would do well to be familiar with the differences between ICD-9 and DSM-III. The most striking differences are the smaller number of diagnostic entities and the absence of operational criteria for disorders in ICD-9.

On Axis I there are significant differences that should be noted. Below is reprinted a description of ICD-9/U.K. Axis I.

FIRST AXIS: CLINICAL PSYCHIATRIC SYNDROME

The first axis consists of Section V of ICD-9 except that the codes for specific delays in development (315) have been removed to constitute a separate second axis; and that the codes for mental retardation (317–319) have been removed to constitute a separate third axis. Otherwise the organisation of codings and their glossary descriptions are unchanged.

It is a principle of the ICD that there should not be different classifications for different age groups (although there must be and is provision for disorders arising only at particular age periods). As a consequence, the first axis includes codings for disorders which have little relevance for children. To facilitate reference, the index highlights categories which are likely to be commonly used in child psychiatry.

The glossary provides descriptions for all categories but certain general points require emphasis. First, if child psychiatric disorders can be included under one of the headings used with adult conditions, that code should be used. Thus, if a child has an anxiety neurosis which fits the description provided for 300.0, that is the coding which should be made. The coding for "disturbance of emotions specific to childhood and adolescence" (313) should be employed only when the disorder is not included in the 300 codings and is of a type characteristic of the childhood period.

Second, although the classification is based on the principle that assumptions of aetiology should be avoided, an aetiological statement has been retained in categories 291 (alcoholic psychoses) and 292 (drug psychoses) since many authorities wish to be able to identify these conditions at the 3-digit level for public health reasons. All other disorders are defined in terms of phenomenology with the exception of 308 (acute reaction to stress) and 309 (adjustment reaction) in which the main criteria refer to the duration and/or the mildness of the disorders. The codings of 307 and 309 should be used only when the disorders meet these criteria and should *not* be employed simply because environmental influences are thought to be important in aetiology. Their relevance is catered for in axis five.

It should be noted that depressive disorders may be coded in several different places. Those which are psychotic or likely to be severe are catered for under 296 (affective psychoses), 298 (other non-organic psychoses largely or entirely reactive to a recent life experience) and 308 (acute reaction to stress). Those which are neurotic or likely to be of mild or moderate degree are provided for in subcategories under 300 (neurotic disorders), 309 (adjustment reaction) and 311 (depressive disorder, not elsewhere classified). In addition, disorders involving depressive symptomatology may be coded under 313.1 (disturbance of emotions specific to childhood and adolescence), 312.3 (mixed disturbance of conduct and emotions) and 301.1 (affective personality disorder).

It may be seen that a distinction is drawn between drug dependence (304) and non-dependent abuse of drugs (305).

Finally, it may be noted that there is a special coding (316) to record mental disturbances or psychic factors which are thought to have played a major part in the aetiology of physical conditions involving tissue damage (such as asthma or peptic ulcer). If a coding of 316 is made the physical condition should always be coded separately on the fourth axis. Physical conditions which do not involve tissue damage but are thought to result from psychic factors eg. psychogenic hiccup or pruritus, should be coded under 306.

ICD-9/UK AXIS I DISORDERS USUALLY OCCURRING IN INFANCY, CHILDHOOD OR ADOLESCENCE

The Axis I disorders of ICD-9 relevant to child practitioners are characterized by several important differences from the childhood section of DSM-III. For one, there are fewer ICD-9 Axis I categories. In addition, ICD-9 urges a *single* Axis I diagnosis, as opposed to DSM-III's encouragement of multiple coding. (E.g., a child would not receive a diagnosis of both Conduct Disorder and Hyperkinetic syndrome of childhood.) Instead, where DSM-III would urge multiple coding, ICD-9 has categories which describe the mixed nature of the disorder and such coding is appropriate when the significant feature of the case includes two types of disturbances. These categories are heavily used in application of the ICD-9 system (i.e., mixed disturbance of emotions and conduct). A more specific difference between types of disorders is the ICD-9 class of conduct disorder. It is not as restrictive as in DSM-III, where the nature of the antisocial acts is specified.

The following Axis I disorders are included because of their proximity to the DSM-III description of childhood disorders.

299. PSYCHOSES WITH ORIGIN SPECIFIC TO CHILDHOOD

This category should be used only for psychoses which always begin before puberty. *Adult type psychoses such as schizophrenia or manic-depressive psychoses when occurring in childhood should be coded elsewhere under the appropriate heading*—i.e. 295 and 296 for the examples given.

.0 Infantile Autism

A syndrome present from birth or beginning almost invariably in the first 30 months. Responses to auditory and sometimes to visual stimuli are abnormal and there are usually severe problems in the understanding of spoken language. Speech is delayed, and if it develops, is characterized by echolalia, the reversal of pronouns, immature grammatical structure and inability to use abstract terms. There is generally an impairment in the social use of both verbal and gestural language. Problems in social relationships are most severe before the age of five years and include an impairment in the development of eye to eye gaze, social attachments, and cooperative play. Ritualistic behaviour is usual and may include abnormal routines, resistance to change, attachment to odd objects and stereotyped patterns of play. The capacity for abstract or symbolic thought and for imaginative play is diminished. Intelligence ranges from severely subnormal to normal or above. Performance is usually better on tasks involving rote memory or visuospatial skills than on those requiring symbolic or linguistic skills.

Childhood autism   Kanner's syndrome
Infantile psychosis

Excludes: disintegrative psychosis or Heller's syndrome (299.1)
              schizophrenic syndrome of childhood (299.9)

.1 Disintegrative Psychosis
Disorders in which normal or near normal development for the first few years is followed by a loss of social skills and of speech, together with a severe disorder of emotions, behaviour and relationships. Usually this loss of speech and of social competence takes place over a period of a few months and is accompanied by the emergence of overactivity and of stereotypies. In most cases there is intellectual impairment, but this is not a necessary part of the disorder. The condition may follow overt brain disease—such as measles, encephalitis—but also it may occur in the absence of any known organic brain disease or damage. Use additional code to identify any associated neurological disorder.

Heller's syndrome

Excludes: Infantile autism (299.0)
              schizophrenic syndrome of childhood (299.9)

Neurotic Disorders, Personality Disorders and other Non-psychotic Mental Disorders (300–316)

300. NEUROTIC DISORDERS
The distinction between neurosis and psychosis is difficult and remains subject to debate. However, it has been retained in view of its wide usage.

Neurotic disorders are mental disorders without any demonstrable organic basis in which the patient may have considerable insight and has unimpaired reality testing, in that he usually does not confuse his morbid subjective experiences and fantasies with external reality. Behaviour may be greatly affected although usually remaining within socially acceptable limits, but personality is not disorganized. The principal manifestations include excessive anxiety, hysterical symptoms, phobias, obsessional and compulsive symptoms and depression.

.0 Anxiety States
Various combinations of physical and mental manifestations of anxiety, not attributable to real danger and occurring either in attacks or as a persisting state. The anxiety is usually diffuse and may extend to panic. Other neurotic features such as obsessional or hysterical symptoms may be present but do not dominate the clinical picture.

Anxiety: neurosis   Panic: attack
        reaction   state
        state (neurotic)

Excludes: neurasthenia (300.5)
              psychophysiological disorders (306.–)

.2 Phobic State
Neurotic states with abnormally intense dread of certain objects or specific situations which would not normally have that effect. If the anxiety tends to spread from a specified situation or object to a wider range of circumstances, it becomes akin to or identical with anxiety state, and should be classified as such (300.0).

Anxiety-hysteria   Claustrophobia
Agoraphobia   Phobia NOS
Animal phobias

Excludes: anxiety state (300.0)
              obsessional phobias (300.3)

.3 Obsessive-Compulsive Disorder
States in which the outstanding symptom is a feeling of subjective compulsion—which must be resisted—to carry out some action, to dwell on an idea, to recall an experience, or to ruminate on an abstract topic. Unwanted thoughts which intrude, the insistency of words or ideas, ruminations or trains of thought are perceived by the patient to be inappropriate

or nonsensical. The obsessional urge or idea is recognized as alien to the personality but as coming from within the self. Obsessional actions may be quasi-ritual performances designed to relieve anxiety, e.g. washing the hands to cope with contamination. Attempts to dispel the unwelcome thoughts or urges may lead to a severe inner struggle, with intense anxiety.

Anankastic neurosis
Compulsive neurosis

Excludes: obsessive-compulsive symptoms occurring in:
         endogenous depression (296.1)
         schizophrenia (295.–)
         organic states, e.g. encephalitis

.4 Neurotic Depression

A neurotic disorder characterized by disproportionate depression which has usually recognizably ensued on a distressing experience; it does not include among its features delusions or hallucinations, and there is often preoccupation with the psychic trauma which preceded the illness, e.g. loss of a cherished person or possession. Anxiety is also frequently present and mixed states of anxiety and depression should be included here. The distinction between depressive neuroses and psychoses should be made not only upon the degree of depression but also on the presence or absence of other neurotic and psychotic characteristics and upon the degree of disturbance of the patient's behaviour.

Anxiety depression   Neurotic depressive state
Depressive reaction   Reactive depression
Neurotic depression

Excludes: adjustment reaction with depressive symptoms (309.0)
         depression NOS (311)
         manic-depressive psychosis, depressed type (296.1)
         reactive depressive psychosis (298.0)

307. SPECIAL SYMPTOMS OR SYNDROMES NOT ELSEWHERE CLASSIFIED

Conditions in which an outstanding symptom or group of symptoms is not manifestly part of a more fundamental classifiable condition.

Excludes: when due to mental disorders classified elsewhere when of organic origin

.0 Stammering and Stuttering

Disorders in the rhythm of speech in which the individual knows precisely what he wishes to say, but at the time is unable to say it because of an involuntary, repetitive prolongation or cessation of a sound.

Excludes: dysphasia (781.5)
lisping or lalling (307.9)
retarded development of speech (314.3)

.1 Anorexia Nervosa

Disorders in which the main features are persistent active refusal to eat and marked loss of weight. The level of activity and alertness is characteristically high in relation to the degree of emaciation. Typically the disorder begins in teenage girls but it may sometimes begin before puberty and rarely it occurs in males. Amenorrhoea is usual and there may be a variety of other physiological changes including slow pulse and respiration, low body temperature and dependent oedema. Unusual eating habits and attitudes toward food are typical and sometimes starvation follows or alternates with periods of overeating. The accompanying psychiatric symptoms are diverse.

Excludes: eating disturbance NOS (307.5)
loss of appetite (784.0)
of non-organic origin (307.5)

.2 Tics

Disorders of no known organic origin in which the outstanding feature consists of quick, involuntary apparently purposeless and frequently repeated movements which are not due to any neurological condition. Any part of the body may be involved but the face is most frequently affected. Only one form of tic may be present, or there may be a combination of tics which are carried out simultaneously, alternatively or consecutively. Gilles de la Tourette's syndrome refers to a rare disorder occurring in individuals of any level of intelligence in which facial tics and tic-like throat noises become more marked and more generalized and in which later, whole words or short sentences (often with an obscene content) are ejaculated spasmodically and involuntarily. There is some overlap with other varieties of tic.

Excludes: nail biting or thumb sucking (307.9)
stereotypies occurring in isolation (307.3)
tics of organic origin (333.3)

.3 Stereotyped Repetitive Movements
Disorders in which voluntary repetitive stereotyped movements, which are not due to any psychiatric or neurological condition, constitute the main feature. Includes head-banging, spasmus nutans, rocking, twirling, finger-flicking mannerisms and eye poking. Such movements are particularly common in cases of mental retardation with sensory impairment or with environmental monotony.

Stereotypies NOS

Excludes: tics:
>   NOS (307.2)
>   of organic origin (333.3)

4. Specific Disorders of Sleep
This category should only be used when a more precise medical or psychiatric diagnosis cannot be made.

Hypersomnia
Insomnia
Inversion of sleep rhythm
Nightmares
Night terrors
Sleepwalking

} of non-organic origin

Excludes: narcolepsy (347.0)
>   when of unspecified cause (780.5)

.5 Other Disorders of Eating
This category should only be used when a more precise medical or psychiatric diagnosis cannot be made.

Infantile feeding disturbances
Loss of appetite
Overeating
Pica
Psychogenic vomiting

} of non-organic origin

Excludes: anorexia:
>   nervosa (307.1)
>   of unspecified cause (785.0)

overeating, of unspecified cause (277.9)
vomiting:
NOS (785.2)
cyclical (536.2)
psychogenic (306.4)

.6 Enuresis

Disorders in which the main manifestation is a persistent involuntary voiding of urine by day or night which is considered abnormal for the age of the individual. Sometimes the child will have failed to gain bladder control and in other cases he will have gained control and then lost it. Episodic or fluctuating enuresis should be included. The disorder would not usually be diagnosed under the age of four years.

Enuresis (primary) (secondary) of non-organic origin

Excludes: when of unspecified cause (787.3)

.7 Encopresis

Disorders in which the main manifestation is the persistent voluntary or involuntary passage of formed motions of normal or near-normal consistency into places not intended for that purpose in the individual's own socio-cultural setting. Sometimes the child has failed to gain bowel control and sometimes he has gained control, but then later again became encopretic. There may be a variety of associated psychiatric symptoms and there may be smearing of faeces. The condition would not usually be diagnosed under the age of four years.

Encopresis (continuous) (discontinuous) of non-organic origin

Excludes: when of unspecified cause (786.5)

309. ADJUSTMENT REACTION

Mild or transient disorders lasting longer than acute stress reactions (308) which occur in individuals of any age without any apparent pre-existing mental disorder. Such disorders are often relatively circumscribed or situation-specific, are generally reversible and usually last only a few months. They are usually closely related in time and content to stresses such as bereavement, migration or separation experiences. Reactions to major stress that last longer than a few days are also included here. In children such disorders are associated with no significant distortion of development.

Excludes: acute reaction to major stress (308.–)
neurotic disorders (300.–)

.0 Brief Depressive Reaction
States of depression, not specifiable as manic-depressive, psychotic or neurotic, generally transient, in which the depressive symptoms are usually closely related in time and content to some stressful event.

Grief reaction

Excludes: affective psychoses (296.–)
neurotic depression (300.4)
prolonged depressive reaction (309.1)
psychogenic depressive psychosis (298.0)

.1 Prolonged Depressive Reaction
States of depression, not specifiable as manic-depressive, psychotic or neurotic, generally long-lasting; usually developing in association with prolonged exposure to a stressful situation.

Excludes: affective psychoses (296.–)
brief depressive reaction (309.0)
neurotic depression (300.4)
psychogenic depressive psychosis (298.0)

.2 With Predominant Disturbance of Other Emotions
States fulfilling the general criteria for adjustment reaction, in which the main symptoms are emotional in type (anxiety, fear, worry etc.) but not specifically depressive.

Culture shock   Abnormal separation anxiety

.3 With Predominant Disturbance of Conduct
Mild or transient disorders, fulfilling the general criteria for adjustment reaction, in which the main disturbance predominantly involves a disturbance of conduct. For example an adolescent grief reaction resulting in aggressive or antisocial disorder would be included here.

Excludes: disturbance of conduct NOS (312.–)
personality disorder with predominantly sociopathic or aso-

cial manifestations (301.7)
dyssocial behaviour without manifest psychiatric disorder

.4 With Mixed Disturbance of Emotions and Conduct
Disorders fulfilling the general definition in which both emotional disturbance and disturbance of conduct are prominent features.

312. DISTURBANCE OF CONDUCT NOT ELSEWHERE CLASSIFIED
Disorders mainly involving aggressive and destructive behaviour *and* disorders involving delinquency. It should be used for abnormal behaviour, in individuals of any age, which gives rise to social disapproval but which is not part of any other psychiatric condition. Minor emotional disturbances may also be present. To be included, the behaviour—as judged by its frequency, severity and type of associations with other symptoms— must be abnormal in its context. Disturbances of conduct are distinguished from an adjustment reaction by a longer duration and by a lack of close relationship in time and content to some stress. They differ from a personality disorder by the absence of deeply ingrained maladaptive patterns of behaviour present from adolescence or earlier.

Excludes: adjustment reaction with disturbance of conduct (309.3)
drug dependence (304.–)
personality disorder with predominantly sociopathic or asocial manifestations (301.7)
sexual deviation (302.–)
dyssocial behaviour without manifest psychiatric disorder

.0 Unsocialized Disturbance of Conduct
Disorders characterized by behaviours such as defiance, disobedience, quarrelsomeness, aggression, destructive behaviour, tantrums, solitary stealing, lying, teasing, bullying and disturbed relationships with others. The defiance may sometimes take the form of sexual misconduct.

Unsocialized aggressive disorder.

.1 Socialized Disturbance of Conduct
Disorders in individuals who have acquired the values of behaviour of a delinquent peer group to whom they are loyal and with whom they characteristically steal, play truant, and stay out late at night. There may also be promiscuity.

Group delinquency.

Excludes: gang activity without manifest psychiatric disorder

.2 Compulsive Conduct Disorder
Cases in which the disorder of conduct or delinquent act is specifically compulsive in origin.

Kleptomania

.3 Mixed Disturbance of Conduct and Emotions
Disorders involving behaviours listed for 312.0 and 312.1 but in which there is also *considerable* emotional disturbance as shown for example by anxiety, misery or obsessive manifestations.

Neurotic delinquency

Excludes: compulsive conduct disorder (312.2)

313. DISTURBANCE OF EMOTIONS SPECIFIC TO CHILDHOOD AND ADOLESCENCE
Less well differentiated emotional disorders characteristic of the childhood period. Where the emotional disorder takes the form of a neurotic disorder described under 300, the appropriate 300 coding should be made. This category differs from category 308 in terms of longer duration and by the lack of close relationship in time and content to some stress.

Excludes: adjustment reaction (309.-)
masturbation, nail biting, thumb sucking and other isolated symptoms (307.-)

.0 With Anxiety and Fearfulness
Ill-defined emotional disorders characteristic of childhood in which the main symptoms involve anxiety and fearfulness. Many cases of school refusal or elective mutism might be included here.

Overanxious reaction of childhood or adolescence

Excludes: abnormal separation anxiety (309.2)
anxiety states (300.0)
hospitalism in children (309.8)
phobic state (300.2)

.1 With Misery and Unhappiness
Emotional disorders characteristic of childhood in which the main symptoms involve misery and unhappiness. There may also be eating and sleep disturbances.

Excludes: depressive neurosis (300.4)

.2 With Sensitivity, Shyness and Social Withdrawal
Emotional disorders characteristic of childhood in which the main symptoms involve sensitivity, shyness, or social withdrawal. Some cases of elective mutism might be included here.

Withdrawing reaction of childhood or adolescence

Excludes: infantile autism (299.0)
          schizoid personality (301.2)
          schizophrenia (295.–)

.3 Relationship Problems
Emotional disorders characteristic of childhood in which the main symptoms involve relationship problems.

Sibling jealousy

Excludes: relationship problems associated with aggression, destruction or other forms of conduct disturbance (312.–)

.8 Other or Mixed
Many emotional disorders of childhood include several elements but whenever possible a specific coding under .0, .1, .2 or .3 should be made according to the *preponderant* type of disturbance. The category of mixed disorders should only be used when there is such an admixture that this cannot be done.

314. HYPERKINETIC SYNDROME OF CHILDHOOD
Disorders in which the essential features are short attention span and distractibility. In early childhood the most striking symptom is disinhibited, poorly organized and poorly regulated extreme overactivity but in adolescence this may be replaced by underactivity. Impulsiveness, marked mood fluctuations and aggression are also common symptoms. Delays in the development of specific skills are often present and disturbed peer re-

lationships are common. If the hyperkinesis is symptomatic of an underlying disorder, code the underlying disorder as well.

.0 Simple Disturbance of Activity and Attention
Cases in which short attention span, distractibility, and overactivity are the main manifestations without significant disturbance of conduct or delay in specific skills.

Overactivity NOS

.1 Hyperkinesis with Developmental Delay
Cases in which the hyperkinetic syndrome is associated with speech delay, clumsiness, reading difficulties or other delays in specific skills.

Developmental disorder of hyperkinesis
Use additional code to identify any associated neurological disorder

.2 Hyperkinetic Conduct Disorder
Cases in which the hyperkinetic syndrome is associated with marked conduct disturbance but not developmental delay.

Hyperkinetic conduct disorder

Excludes: with significant delays in specific skills (314.1)

ICD-9/U.K. AXIS V
This fifth axis, Abnormal Psychosocial Situations, is included because of its useful description of situations implying particular importance in the diagnosis of childhood disorders.

AXIS FIVE: ASSOCIATED ABNORMAL PSYCHOSOCIAL SITUATIONS

Principles
This axis concerns aspects of the patient's current psychosocial situation which are markedly abnormal in the *context* of the patient's level of development and socio-cultural circumstances. Situations should be coded irrespective of whether they are thought to have directly caused psychiatric disorder. However, situations which are abnormal solely as part of the patient's symptomatology should be excluded.

More than one coding may be made on this axis. If this is done, codings should be put in order of importance with respect to the patient.

GLOSSARY OF TERMS

00. No Significant Distortion or Inadequacy of Psychosocial Environment
Includes: all psychosocial circumstances which are not codeable below. Stresses and adversities of mild degree only (as well as a fully normal psychosocial environment) would be coded here.

01. Mental Disturbance in Other Family Members
Includes: any kind of overt, handicapping psychiatric disorder or any kind of *gross* abnormality of behaviour (*not* necessarily receiving psychiatric treatment) in a member of the patient's immediate household or in a parent or sib of the patient regardless of whether or not they are in the same household.
Excludes: mental retardation in family members if unassociated with behavioral abnormality; psychiatric disorder in more distant relatives.

02. Discordant Intra-Familial Relationships
Includes: discord or disharmony (such as shown by hostility, quarrelling, scapegoating, etc.) of sufficient severity to lead to a persisting atmosphere in the home or to persisting interpersonal tensions. Discordant relationships between the two parents, discordant relationships between parent and patient and discordant relationships with a sib should be included here (irrespective of whether they are living together).
Excludes: lack of warmth or affection (03) if not associated with discord.

03. Lack of Warmth in Intra-familial Relationships
Includes: a *marked* lack of warmth or affection; or a coldness and distance in the relationships between the parents or between parent and patient (irrespective of whether they are living together); lack of empathetic responsiveness as distinct from punitiveness or restrictiveness.
Excludes: discord and disharmony (02) if in the context of warm relationships.

04. Familial Over-Involvement
Includes: a *marked* excess of intrusiveness (such as shown by over-protection, over-restriction, incestuous relationships or undue

emotional stimulation etc.) by another family member when judged in relation to the patient's maturity level and the socio-familial context.

Excludes: increased control which is appropriate to the patient's developmental level and behaviour.

05. Inadequate or Inconsistent Parental Control

Includes: a *marked* lack of effective control or supervision of the patient's activities when judged in relation to the patient's maturity level and the socio-familial context. *Markedly* inconsistent or inefficient discipline should be coded here.

06. Inadequate Social, Linguistic or Perceptual Stimulation

Includes: a *marked* lack of effective and meaningful social, linguistic *or* perceptual experiences when judged in relation to the patient's developmental needs; whether arising as a result of inadequate or inappropriate parent-child interaction, periods of poor quality substitute care, or for any other reason. A marked lack of toys, a failure to engage the child in adequate play or conversation, or a gross isolation from other children would be included. An institutional upbringing which provided adequate cognitive stimulation but a marked lack of affective ties should also be coded here.

07. Inadequate Living Conditions

Includes: *grossly* inadequate living conditions, however caused. Marked poverty, lack of basic household amenities (bath, hot running water, etc.), overcrowding (to the extent of at least 1–5 persons per all rooms used for living, dining or sleeping), shared beds, vermin infestation of home, and severe damp would all be included.

08. Inadequate or Distorted Intra-Familial Communication

Includes: a *marked* lack or distortion of communication or discussion between family members of such severity that important family issues are either not discussed or are the subject of misleading messages between family members.

Excludes: quarrelsome interchanges which nevertheless allow adequate discussion of important issues even if negative feelings prevent their resolution (02).

09. Anomalous Family Situation

Includes: an institutional environment (other than that arising from a limited episode of hospital care), single parent family, upbringing by a homosexual couple, fostering, or multiple parenting when there is no immediate family context.

Excludes: *past* separations or break-up of the family unless associated with a currently anomalous family situation; upbringing by a married couple one or both of whom are not biologically related to the child; communal upbringing when there is also a family group.

10. Stresses or Disturbances in School or Work Environment

Includes: any *marked* acute or chronic stress or disturbance in the person's school or work environment such as that caused by severe interpersonal tensions, bullying, isolation from peers, inability to cope with the work involved, personal loss or marked instability in the school or work environment.

Excludes: disturbances which are solely part of the patient's disorder.

11. Migration or Social Transplantation

Includes: recent migration or movement of the patient to a different socio-cultural environment or any kind of move which results in a severe disruption of personal ties or relationships (such as eviction resulting in break-up of the family or homelessness).

12. Natural Disaster

Includes: any recent disaster impinging on the patient which arises as a result of natural causes which leads to severe social disruption or social disadvantage. Floods, earthquakes, volcanoes, landslides, damage due to storm would all be included.

Excludes: disasters due to war, riot or accident (16).

13. Other Intra-familial Psychosocial Stress

Includes: any recent or current *marked* stress on the patient arising within the family such as caused by bereavement, divorce, or separation; illness, accident or physical handicap of a member of the patient's immediate family; or the departure of a loved person from within the home.

Excludes: acute stresses arising outside the family such as caused by the death of a friend (14) or stresses at school/work (10).

14. Other Extra-Familial Psychosocial Stress

Includes: any recent or current *marked* stress on the patient arising outside the family such as caused by bereavement, illness, accident, broken important relationship, personal rejection, or personal failure.

Excludes: acute stresses arising within the family (13), stresses in the
school or work environment (10).

15. Persecution or Adverse Discrimination

Includes: any kind of persecution or gross adverse discrimination on the
basis of racial, social, religious or other group characteristics
which directly impinges on the patient.

Excludes: bullying or teasing at school or work on the basis of personal
characteristics (10).

16. Other Psychosocial Disturbance in Society in General

Includes: any chronic psychosocial disturbance in society in general
which directly and markedly impinges on the patient. War,
civil unrest, famine, pandemics and other persisting disrup-
tions of social life would be included here.

88. Other (specified)

Includes: any acute or chronic stress, distortion, or disadvantage in a person's psychosocial environment which is not codeable above.

Excludes: physical disabilities (code under axis 4)
intellectual disabilities (code under axis 3)
genetic predisposition (not coded unless associated with a
codeable psychosocial situation on this axis or a codeable medical, intellectual, or developmental condition on other axes).

99. Psychosocial Situation Unknown

Appendix II

Diagnostic Scales and Interviews

PARENT AND TEACHER RATING SCALES

1. *ECDEU Assessment Manual for Psychopharmacology*. DHEW Publication No. (ADM) 76-338, National Institutes of Mental Health; Alcohol, Drug Abuse, and Mental Health Administration (ADAMHA), Bethesda, 1976.
2. Achenbach, T.: The child behavior profile. I. Boys aged 6–11. *J. Consult. Clin. Psychol.*, 1978, 46:478–488.
3. Achenbach, T., & Edelbrock, C.: The child behavior profile. II. Boys aged 12–16 and girls aged 6–11 and 12–16. *J. Consult. Clin. Psychol.*, 1979, 47:223–233.
4. Achenbach, T.: DSM-III in light of empirical research in the classification of child psychopathology. *J. Am. Acad. Child Psychiat.*, 1980, 19:395–412.
5. Conners, C.: Rating scales for use in drug studies with children. In *Psychopharmacology Bulletin*. (Special Issue—Pharmacotherapy with children), Bethesda, 1973, pp. 24–84.
6. Conners, C.: Rating scales for use in drug studies with children. In *ECDEU Assessment Manual*, Bethesda, 1976, pp. 303–312.
7. CPRS—*ECDEU Assessment Manual*, Bethesda, 1976, pp. 124–129.
8. Orveschol, H., Schalomikas, D., & Weissman, M.: The assessment of psychopathology and behavioral problems in children: A review of scales suitable for epidemiological and clinical research (1967–79). Report for the center for Epidemiologic Studies (Contact # ADM 42-74-83 (DBE)), National Institute of Mental Health; Alcohol, Drug Abuse, and Mental Health Administration (ADAMHA), Bethesda, 1979.
9. Speer, D.: The behavior problem checklist (Peterson-Quay): Baseline data from parents of child guidance and non-clinic children. *J. Consult. Clin. Psychol.*, 1971, 36:221–228.

10. Werry, J., Sprague, R., & Cohen, M.: Conners' teacher rating scale for use in drug studies with children—An empirical study. *J. Abnormal Child Psychol.,* 1975, 3:217–229.

PATIENT INTERVIEWS

1. Diagnostic Interviews Schedule for Children, NIMH-DIS-C. Lenore Radloff, Division of Biometry and Epidemiology, Room 18C-05, Parklawn Building, 5600 Fishers Lane, Bethesda, MD.
2. KIDDIE-SADS. Joaquim Puig-Antich, M.D., Psychiatric Institute, 722 W. 168th Street, New York, NY.
3. ISC—Interview Schedule for Children. Maria Kovves, Ph.D., Department of Psychiatry, University of Pittsburgh, School of Medicine, Pittsburgh, PA.

References

Achenbach, T.: The child behavior profile: An empirically based system for assessing children's behavioral problems and competencies. *Int. J. Ment. Health*, 1979, 7:24–42.

Achenbach, T., & Edelbrock, C.: The classifications of child psychopathology: A review and analysis of empirical effects. *Psychological Bulletin*, 1978, 85:1275–1301.

Bradley, C.: The behavior of children receiving benzedrine. *Am. J. of Orthopsychiatry*, 1937, 94:577–585.

Campbell, M., Geller, B., & Cohen, I.: Current status of drug research and treatment with autistic children. *J. Ped. Psychol.*, 1977, 2:153–161.

Cantor, S., Evans, J., Pearce, J., & Pezzot-Pearce, T.: Childhood schizophrenia: Present but not accounted for. *Am. J. Psychiat.*, 1982, 139(6):758–762.

Cantwell, D., Russell, A., Mattison, R., & Will, L.: A comparison of DSM-II and DSM-III in the diagnosis of childhood psychiatric disorders: I. Agreement with expected diagnosis. *Arch. Gen. Psychiat.*, 1979, 36:1208–1213. (a)

Cantwell, D., Russell, A., Mattison, R., & Will, L.: A comparison of DSM-II and DSM-III in the diagnosis of childhood psychiatric disorders: IV. Difficulties in use, global comparisons and conclusions. *Arch. Gen. Psychiat.*, 1979, 36:1227–1228. (b)

Carlson, G., & Cantwell, D.: Diagnosis of childhood depression: A comparison of Weinberg and DSM-III Criteria. *J. Am. Acad. Child Psychiat.*, 1982, 21:247–250.

Close, J.: Manual for the neurological examination for soft signs. In *ECDEU Assessment Manual*, 1976, pp. 394–406.

Conners, C.: A teacher rating scale for use in drug studies with children. *Am. J. Psychiat.*, 1969, 126:884–888.

Conners, C.: Symptom patterns in hyperkinetic, neurotic, and normal children. *Child Development*, 1970, 41:667–682.

Creak, M.: Schizophrenic syndrome in childhood. *Dev. Medicine in Child Neurology*, 1964, 6:530–535.

Dyson, L., & Barcai, A.: Treatment of lithium responding patients. *Curr. Ther. Res.*, 1970, 12:286–290.

Earls, T.: Application of DSM-III in an epidemiological study of preschool children. *Am. J. Psychiat.*, 1982, 139:242–243.

Fish, B.: Neurobiologic antecedents of schizophrenia in children. *Arch. Gen. Psychiat.*, 1977, 37:1297–1313.

157

Gittelman, R.: The role of psychological tests for differential diagnosis in child psychiatry. *J. Am. Acad. Child Psychiat.*, 1980, 19:413–438.

Gittelman-Klein, R., Spitzer, R., & Cantwell, D.: Diagnostic classifications and psychopharmacological indications. In J. Werry (Ed.), *Pediatric Psychopharmacology: The Use of Behavior Modifying Drugs in Children.* New York: Brunner/Mazel, 1978.

Goldman, J., Stein, C. L., & Guerry, S.: *Psychological Methods of Child Assessment.* New York: Brunner/Mazel, 1984.

Group for the Advancement of Psychiatry (GAP): *Psychopathological Disorders in Childhood.* New York: Jason Aronson, 1974.

Kanner, L.: *Child Psychiatry.* Springfield, IL: Charles C Thomas, 1935.

Kanner, L.: *Child Psychiatry.* (3rd Edition). Springfield, IL: Charles C Thomas, 1962, pp. 726–751.

Loney, J., Kramer, J., & Milich, R.: The hyperkinetic child grows up: Predictors of symptoms, delinquency and achievement at follow-up. In K. Gadow & J. Loney (Eds.), *Psychosocial Aspects of Drug Treatment for Hyperactivity.* Boulder, Colorado: Westview Press, 1981, pp. 381–415.

Mattison, R., Cantwell, D., Russell, A., & Will, L.: A comparison of DSM-II and DSM-III in the diagnosis of childhood psychiatric disorders: II. Interrater agreement. *Arch. Gen. Psychiat.*, 1979, 36:1217–1222.

McKnew, D., Cytryn, L., Buchsbaum, M., Hamovit, J., Lamour, M., Rapoport, J., & Gershon, E.: Lithium response in children of lithium responding parents. *Psychiatry Research*, 1981, 4:171–180.

Nee, L., Caine, E., Polinsky, R., Eldridge, R., & Ebert, M.: Gilles de la Tourette syndrome: A clinical and family study of fifty cases. *Ann. Neurol.*, 1980, 1, 7:41–49.

O'Leary, K., & Carr, E.: Childhood disorders. In G. Wilson & C. Franks (Eds.), *Contemporary Behavior Therapy: Conceptual Foundations of Clinical Practice.* New York: Guilford Press, 1982.

Ornitz, E., & Ritvo, E.: The syndrome of autism: A critical review. *Am. J. Psychiat.*, 1976, 133, 6:609–621.

Puig-Antich, J.: The use of RDC criteria for major depressive disorder in children and adolescents. *J. Am. Acad. Child Psychiat.*, 1982, 21:291–293.

Robins, L. N.: *Deviant Children Grown Up.* Baltimore: Williams and Wilkins, 1966.

Russell, A., Cantwell, D., Mattison, R., & Will, L.: A comparison of DSM-II and DSM-III in the diagnosis of childhood psychiatric disorders: III. Multiaxial features. *Arch. Gen. Psychiat.*, 1979, 36:1223–1226.

Rutter, M., Lebovici, S., Eisenberg, L., Snezvenskij, A., Sadoun, R., Brooke, E., & Lin, T.: A triaxial classification of mental disorders in childhood. *J. Child Psychol. Psychiat.*, 1979, 10:41–61.

Rutter, M., & Schopler, E.: *Autism.* New York: Plenum Press, 1978.

Rutter, M., & Shaffer, D.: DSM-III—A step forward or back in terms of the classification of child psychiatric disorders? *J. Am. Acad. Child Psychiat.*, 1980, 19:371–394.

Rutter, M., Shaffer, D., & Shepherd, M.: *A Multiaxial Classification of Child Psychiatric Disorders.* Geneva: World Health Organization, 1975.

Rutter, M., Tizard, J., & Whitmore, K.: *Education, Health and Behavior: Psychological and Medical Study of Childhood Development.* New York: John Wiley, 1970.

Shapiro, A., Shapiro, E., & Wayne, H.: Treatment of Tourette's syndrome. *Arch. Gen. Psychiat.*, 1973, 28:92–97.

Spitzer, R., & Cantwell, D.: The DSM-III classification of psychiatric disorders of infancy, childhood and adolescence. *J. Am. Acad. Child Psychiat.*, 1980, 19:356–370.

Sprague, R., & Baxley, G. Drugs for behavior management, with comment on some legal aspects. In J. Wortis (Ed.), *Mental Retardation and Developmental Disabilities, Vol. X,* New York: Brunner/Mazel, 1978.

Stephens, R., Bartley, L., Rapoport, J., & Berg, C.: A brief preschool playroom interview: Correlates with independent behavioral reports. *J. Am. Acad. Child Psychiat.*, 1980, 19: 213–224.

Weiner, J. (Ed.): *Psychopharmacology in Childhood and Adolescence.* New York: Basic Books, 1977.

Welner, A., Welner, Z., & Fishman, R.: Psychiatric adolescent inpatients: Eight to ten year follow-up. *Arch. Gen. Psychiat.*, 1979, 36:698–700.

Werry, J. (Ed.): *Pediatric Psychopharmacology: The Use of Behavior Modifying Drugs in Children.* New York: Brunner/Mazel, 1978.

Wolff, S.: Symptomatology and outcome of preschool children with behavior disorders attending a child guidance clinic. *J. Child Psychol. Psychiat.*, 1961, 2:269–276.

Index

161